WARRIOR SPIRIT

Warrior Spirit

The Story of Native American Patriotism and Heroism

HERMAN J. VIOLA

Foreword by Debra Kay Mooney

Contributions by Ellen Baumler, Cheryl Hughes, and Michelle Pearson

UNIVERSITY OF OKLAHOMA PRESS : NORMAN

This book is published with the generous assistance of the Kerr Foundation, Inc.

Content adapted from *Warriors in Uniform* by Herman J. Viola and *Counting Coup* by Joseph Medicine Crow and Herman J. Viola. Used by permission of National Geographic Partners, LLC. All rights reserved.

Library of Congress Cataloging-in-Publication Data

Names: Viola, Herman J., author.
Title: Warrior spirit : the story of Native American heroism and patriotism / Herman J. Viola ; foreword by Debra Kay Mooney ; contributions by Ellen Baumler, Cheryl Hughes and Michelle Pearson.
Description: Norman : University of Oklahoma Press, [2022] | Includes bibliographical references and index. | Audience: Grades 10–12 | Summary: "Highlights the military service and sacrifices of Native American soldiers and veterans in the U.S. Army, from the Revolutionary War and the Civil War, through World Wars I and II, to the wars in Vietnam, the Persian Gulf, Afghanistan, and Iraq. Tells the personal wartime stories of Native scouts and soldiers, including Code Talkers. Appropriate for young adult readers"—Provided by publisher.
Identifiers: LCCN 2021032880 | ISBN 978-0-8061-8031-1 (paperback)
Subjects: LCSH: Indian soldiers—History. | Indian soldiers—Biography. | United States—Armed Forces—Indians—History.
Classification: LCC E98.M5 V555 2022 | DDC 355.0089/97073—dc23
LC record available at https://lccn.loc.gov/2021032880

The paper in this book meets the guidelines for permanence and durability of the Committee on Production Guidelines for Book Longevity of the Council on Library Resources, Inc. ∞

To American Indians everywhere,
especially those who have enriched my life
by allowing me to be a part of theirs

CONTENTS

You are about to embark on a journey that will take you to a place where you will be able to see the footsteps of our Native American struggle and understand our culture and our contributions to the armed forces and the United States. The book that will take you on that journey is written by a man who is generous in spirit and supportive of all those around him. I have had the honor of working with Herman Viola on many Native and military projects. Storytelling is a long-held tradition of the Native people. With the onset of the written word it immortalized our cultures and has kept, and will keep, our stories going for many generations.

With a historian like Dr. Viola, with his tireless dedication to the truth, this project can stand on its own merit. You will learn about many tribes and the wars they fought in for this country—at a time when most were not even citizens. The journey is not just an educational one: it will engage your emotions as well.

As you complete this journey, you will see toward the back of the book a photo of the monument dedicated to Native American veterans. It was designed by Harvey Pratt, a Native Marine Corps veteran who served in Vietnam. You will learn all that it took to get the monument actually made. To change your journey from one of reading and imagination to one of action, I urge you to make the trip to Washington, DC, to visit this monument in the courtyard of the National Museum of the American Indian.

Thank you so much for this opportunity to introduce you to *Warrior Spirit*.

Debra Kay Mooney
Choctaw Nation
Retired Army Sergeant First Class

Warbonnets adorn uniform jackets at a Kiowa Black Leggings
Society ceremony, making for an appropriate blending of two
cultures with the warrior tradition that is so much a part of both
worlds. Courtesy National Museum of the American Indian.

Our Enemies Are Crying

Most Americans know little more about our nation's Native peoples than that they hosted a Thanksgiving dinner for the Pilgrims and that Navajos were Code Talkers in World War II. The reason for this ignorance is the failure to teach our students about the important contributions American Indians have made to the success and growth of the United States. What students do learn about Indians is that they were mainly adversaries—not friends, allies, or patriots. In fact, American Indians have fought in uniform in each of our nation's wars even though most of them did not become US citizens until after World War I. This service began in 1775 when the Stockbridge Indians of Massachusetts joined the rebellion against Great Britain. The following year, the Continental Congress gave formal approval to General George Washington to enlist up to two thousand Native Americans because, as he told the Congress, they would make "excellent" scouts and light troops.

Since then, despite a legacy of broken treaties, cultural suppression, and racial discrimination, not only have Indians served, but they continue to serve in numbers that, per capita, far exceed their small percentage of the US population. Why, then, do Indians willingly serve a country that has historically treated them so poorly? When asked this question, Indian veterans invariably answer that they are a warrior people who have a sacred obligation to defend their homeland and their families. That is why, on Veterans Day 2020, the National Museum of the American Indian unveiled on its grounds *The Warriors' Circle of Honor*, a memorial to honor the largely unknown and unrecognized service and sacrifice of Native Americans in the United States military.

Most Americans and the rest of the world may not know about the legacy of Native patriotism and heroism, but the opposite is true in Indian Country. All Indian people take special pride in their veterans. The women actively promote and participate in commemorative events, including traditional dances and parades, while Indian veterans are honored and admired in their home communities to a far greater extent than in other American communities. Visit any reservation and you will be struck by the number of American flags and Veterans of Foreign War (VFW) posts. Indians are not only intensely patriotic but also proud to wear the uniform and celebrate those who wear it, because military service continues age-old traditions that unify the entire community and reinforce the hallowed warrior spirit. This is why Indian veterans are among the most honored members of their communities. They are celebrated before they leave for military service and upon their return, often with ceremonial songs like this one of the Crow Nation:

Our Enemies Are Crying

Isshe'ele Uuwateesh Iiweek.	The Ones with Metal on the Top of the Head [the Lakota] are crying.
Ikku'pe Uuwateesh Iiweek.	The Metal Hats [the Germans of World War I and II] are crying.
Chee'tbachee Pu'mmeesh Iiweek.	The Short Wolf Men [the Asians of World War II, Korea, and Vietnam] are crying.
Ishbi'tchia Lu'sshiash Iiweek	The Curved Knives [the Arabs of the Gulf War, Lebanon, Afghanistan, and Iraq] are crying.
Alawachee' Waatcha'achik Huuash Iiweek	We heard that he was an outstanding man [the enemy soldier] but he is crying

In prereservation days, Indian boys experienced vigorous training, from childhood on, in running, swimming, archery, tracking, horseback riding, hunting, and other related skills. The rigors of nomadic life made Plains Indian people naturally athletic, and they enjoyed sports and games. They were also often at war with neighboring tribes, so at their core they were a warrior people. Among the Crow people, for example, a man's prestige depended on his military record. As Joseph Medicine Crow explains in his book *From the Heart of the Crow Country*, in order to become a chief, a warrior had to perform four difficult deeds called "coups" in combat. But for tribal people, war was not waged to gain property or territory through conquest. To them war was sport—a game of wits, chivalry, bravery, and honor between tribes. Raids on enemy villages were typically performed by teenagers whose boyhood training would thereby be tested in real combat, which meant being a warrior was a young man's sport. By the time warriors reached their thirties, they were considered too old to leave on raids and were tasked instead with protecting their encampments or villages.

Most tribes, especially on the Great Plains, had military clubs or warrior sodalities, like the Kiowa Black Leggings Society featured in this book, that aspiring young warriors sought to join. Retired war chiefs governed their tribes with the assistance of these societies, which performed disciplinary and ceremonial duties as well as military activities. After the tribes were placed on reservations at the close of the nineteenth century, many of the military societies ceased to exist, but some of them, including the Black Leggings, were restored during World War II. Their membership was now made up of US servicemen and veterans who received military names and war songs in accordance with the societies' traditional customs.

Not all tribes glorify warfare, even though they honor their soldiers. For some, especially the Pueblo peoples of the Southwest, there is conflict between being a soldier and the possibility of taking another human's life. This was well expressed in an interview with Cliff Qotsaquahu, then commander of American Legion Hopi Post 80. "Hopis are very reserved in talking about their combat experiences," he said. "They think, how can I be a good Hopi knowing that I possibly killed somebody or did kill somebody? How can I blend the White man's military purpose with the Hopi culture? The Hopi soldiers, like soldiers from other tribes, can get some solace from traditional cleansing ceremonies. For the Hopi it is a rebirth similar to the naming ceremonies. The aunts of the veteran on the paternal side escort the veteran into the village where they wash his hair, give him a new name, cleansing his body and soul of all the taint of combat," Qotsaquahu said. "That's the first step. They can also go to a spiritual leader who will perform rituals of cleansing that last up to four days. If the memories keep coming around, you can do it periodically. But there are no statues among the Hopi for those killed in combat. We don't memorialize them. We believe that they have joined the Cloud People Society and that someday we will join them." (The interview appeared in the Phoenix *Arizona Republic* in May 2003.)

Contrary to popular belief, Indians do not have an innate warrior spirit. It is a learned behavior, not a genetic inheritance. The idea of Indians being "supersoldiers" is a centuries-old stereotype that persists to this day. Because of that belief, Indian soldiers have often been sent to the battlefront or assigned dangerous missions such as serving as scouts and messengers. As Joseph Medicine Crow, whose military exploits during World War II are told in chapter 5, admitted, he was often given dangerous assignments because he was an Indian. "I did them, but I was more scared than the white boys." A sad consequence for Indian soldiers striving to live up to the unrealistic expectations of their supposed "warrior skills" is that they suffered more casualties than their white comrades in combat. For example, during World War I an estimated 5 percent of the Indian doughboys were killed or wounded, as compared to a 1 percent casualty rate for the entire American Expeditionary Force, which suffered a total of 50,280 killed and 95,786 wounded. Some tribal groups suffered even higher rates. An estimated 14 percent of the Pawnee soldiers became casualties, while the various Sioux groups suffered an average casualty rate of 10 percent.

The high casualty rate should not be surprising, says historian Thomas A. Britten, author of *American Indians in World War I*, "given their often perilous duties as scouts, snipers, and messengers." In truth, US Army officers who believed romantic notions of Native American fighting abilities often gave their Indian soldiers the most dangerous assignments. Some Indians, in turn, accepted those assignments to prove their worth as soldiers and to live up to the unrealistic and stereotypical images of their warrior heritage. Nonetheless, some of the Indian soldiers did welcome dangerous duties as opportunities to fulfill their warrior aspirations.

Remarkable as this record of patriotism and military service is, it has largely been overlooked and even ignored by most Americans. President George W. Bush admitted as much when, on March 3, 2008, he awarded the Congressional Medal of Honor to Master Sergeant Woodrow Wilson Keeble for military valor during the Korean War more than twenty-five years after his death. "Some blamed the bureaucracy for a shameful blunder," Bush said. "Others suspected racism. Whatever the reason, the first Sioux Indian ever to receive the Medal of Honor died without knowing it."

Readers of *Warrior Spirit* can follow in the footsteps of Native American veterans as they tell their stories through time, from the first Indian guides and soldiers during the Revolutionary War to the first Indian officer to graduate from West Point, from the soldiers who fought for the North and South in the Civil War, to the tribesmen who served on the battlefields of World Wars I and II, and those who ventured to the distant lands of Vietnam, Iraq, and Afghanistan.

Sources

Britten, Thomas A. *American Indians in World War I: At Home and at War.* Albuquerque: University of New Mexico Press, 1997.

Harris, Alexandra N., and Mark G. Hirsch. *Why We Serve: Native Americans in the United States Armed Forces*. Washington, DC: National Museum of the American Indian, 2020.

Old Horn, Dale. *Music and Dance of the Crow Indians*. Crow Agency, MT: Little Big Horn College, 1999.

Viola, Herman J. *Warriors in Uniform: The Legacy of American Indian Heroism*. Washington, DC: National Geographic Society, 2008.

CHAPTER 1

Peace or Conflict

Until the Civil War finally resolved the issue, America's Native peoples frequently found themselves caught between "two fires." During the American Revolution, Indian loyalty was divided between England and the colonies. During the War of 1812, the choice was between England and the United States. Then, in the Civil War, it was between North and South. Much as the tribes would have preferred to remain neutral in these conflicts, they were often drawn into them, and, for the most part, these conflicts became Native peoples' own civil wars, splitting tribes as well as families.

During the American Revolution, the choice for the Indians was simple and pragmatic: most of their trade goods came from England, while most trespassers on their hunting grounds were colonists. The fact that the Continental Congress offered the Delaware Indians their own state after the Revolution in return for their support indicates the desperation of the colonial cause. This offer, which the Delawares rejected, resembled a clause in a treaty with the Cherokees allowing them to send a representative to Congress. Neither was likely to be accepted by the American public.

The tribes that became most directly involved in the American Revolution were the members of the Iroquois Confederacy. Powerful and primarily pro-British, the confederacy occupied a strategic location along the Hudson River between New England and the Middle Colonies. Of the six tribes in the confederacy, the Seneca, Mohawk, Cayuga, and Onondaga sided with the British. Only the Oneida and Tuscarora took up the Patriot cause.

George Washington, for one, recognized the need for Indian soldiers. They could "be made of excellent use as scouts and light troops," he informed the Continental Congress. Accordingly, the congress in 1786 authorized him to enlist 2,000 Native men. Eventually, of the 250,000 men who served in Washington's army, about 5,500 were Indians.

A number of the Indians who rallied to the Patriot cause were descendants of the so-called "Praying Indians" of New England, whose communities dated from the seventeenth century and the proselytizing activities of the Puritan missionary John Eliot. Now fully assimilated and intermarried with their white and Black neighbors, they little resembled their Mahican, Wappinger, or other tribal ancestors in appearance or culture.

Of these Christian Indians, the residents of Stockbridge, Massachusetts, stand out. Known as the Stockbridge Indians, after their mission village located in the Berkshire Mountains of Massachusetts, the members of this Christian community were primarily Mahican but also included other Native peoples from across New England. The Stockbridge Indians not only used their influence to keep other tribes from supporting the British, but also formed a company in the colonial army and fought in every major campaign in the eastern theater of the American Revolution, from Bunker Hill to the Battle of Monmouth. Their effectiveness as a fighting unit ended in August 1778 when they encountered a unit of the Queen's Rangers, mounted dragoons, near White Plains, New York. Outnumbered five to one, the Indians fought gallantly but were no match for the horsemen who ran them down, killing or disabling some forty of the Mahican patriots and capturing ten. After the battle, local residents buried eighteen Stockbridge soldiers, including their chief, in a site now known as Indian Field in Van Cortlandt Park in the Bronx.

The Oneidas also paid a steep price for their loyalty to the Patriot cause. Like the Praying Indians, the Oneidas were Christian, espousing the Presbyterian tenets of their beloved missionary Samuel Kirkland, a New England Puritan and ardent Patriot. As early as 1775, the Oneidas had organized their own militia company under Captain Tewahangaraghken, or Honyery Doxtator (his English name).

According to his pension file in the National Archives of the United States, he organized a company of Oneida Indians "who were friendly to the Americans in their struggle for liberty and entered the military service of the Revolutionary War." At his side was his wife Tyonajanegen, who, at the Battle of Oriskany Creek, not only handled her own musket but also loaded her husband's gun for him after a ball broke his right wrist. Recalled one white comrade, the Oneidas "fought like Bull dogs."

Oriskany was one of the bloodiest battles of the American Revolution. As many as one-fourth of the eight hundred soldiers in the Patriot ranks died that day. It was also a major factor in the breakup of the Iroquois Confederacy because the battle pitted some sixty Oneidas against an equal force of Mohawks and Senecas led by Mohawk leader Joseph Brant, who held a commission in the British army.

As a result of Oneida support for the Patriot cause, the American Revolution became a civil war for Iroquois as well as for colonial families. One Oneida fighting with the Americans was captured by his own brother, a supporter of the British, who then turned him over to the Senecas for execution.

In the South, the once-powerful Muscogee (Creek) Nation became so divided over colonial-era allegiances that a civil war erupted during the War of 1812 between the "Red Sticks," who sided with the British, and and the "White Sticks," who favored the United States. The breakup of tribal groups in the South presaged the sort of bitter fratricide that would occur during the Civil War, when members of the so-called Five Civilized Tribes joined opposing forces. Although the Indians had little effect on the military outcome of the American Revolution, their participation produced two far-reaching emotional and psychological consequences that shaped white attitudes and US government policy for decades. One was a reputation for brutality inspired by atrocities that are inevitable in every war. The other was the notion that the Indians deserved punishment for siding with the British, even though several tribes cast their lot with the colonies. To make matters worse for the Indians, no matter which side the tribes chose, they all eventually suffered the same racial discrimination and loss of sovereignty after the formation of the United States.

During the War of 1812, when the United States fought its second war of independence from England, Native America again followed diverging courses. On the northern frontier, some Indians rallied to the vision of the Shawnee leader Tecumseh, who called for the tribes to unite against the United States. Tecumseh, a general in the British army, died for his cause while fighting in the Northwest at the Battle of the Thames.

Eventually, Andrew Jackson, with the aid of a Cherokee regiment and the support of the Choctaws led by Chief Pushmataha defeated the Red Sticks at the Battle of Horseshoe Bend in Alabama. Old Hickory (as Jackson was known) then turned his attention to the British. Again drawing upon Indian allies, including five hundred Choctaws, he attacked Pensacola. Jackson's Choctaw allies also aided him later at the Battle of New Orleans. For his loyalty to the American cause, Pushmataha received the brevet commission of brigadier general in the US Army.

Pushmataha, who died on Christmas Eve, 1824, while on a visit to Washington, DC, was rewarded for his loyalty to the United States with a state funeral. His dying wish—for "the big guns to be fired over me"—was honored the day after Christmas by the Marine Corps under the direction of the secretary of the navy and two companies of the District of Columbia militia. Two thousand congressmen, government officials, and citizens followed the cortege led by Andrew Jackson to Congressional Cemetery. The minute guns that thundered on Capitol Hill were echoed by three crisp musket volleys at graveside as the United States paid tribute to the Choctaw general.

No such ceremony honored Major David Moniac, who was killed at the Battle of Wahoo Swamp in 1835 during the Second Seminole War. Of Muscogee and Scottish ancestry, Moniac is considered by many to be the first Native American to graduate from the US Military Academy at West Point. Although other cadets could claim that

PUSHMATAHA

The first Native American general in the US Army is believed to be the Choctaw chief A-Push-ma-ta-ha-hu-bi, commonly known as Pushmataha. His full name translates as "His arm and all the weapons in his hands are fatal to his foes." Pushmataha attained the rank of brevet brigadier general during the War of 1812, when he raised a force of 500 Choctaw soldiers, who served with distinction in various engagements that included the Battle of New Orleans. Popularly known as the "Indian General," he was a strict disciplinarian who was well liked by his fellow officers. They accorded him the status and recognition that befitted his rank on all public, social, and official occasions. General Pushmataha died of pneumonia Christmas Eve, 1824, while in Washington, DC, conducting tribal business. A loyal patriot of the United States his entire life, he once predicted that the Choctaw War Cry would be heard . . . in many foreign lands." It is a prediction that has been fulfilled countless times over as evidenced by the many Choctaw veterans whose stories are told here in *Warrior Spirit*.

Shown here in full military uniform, the Choctaw chief Pushmataha, known as the "Indian General," earned his epaulets fighting for the American cause during the War of 1812. This portrait was painted by Charles Bird King during the chief's visit to Washington, DC, in 1824. Courtesy Herman J. Viola.

distinction because of mixed ancestry, Moniac is the first cadet identified as such in surviving academy records.

Referred to as the "Indian Boy" by Academy superintendent Sylvanus Thayer, the fifteen-year-old Muscogee youngster was admitted in 1817 under the terms of a 1790 treaty between the US government and the Muscogee (Creek) Nation. A secret codicil to that treaty provided that the US government would bear the educational expenses for four Creek men, and the tribe selected David to attend the Academy. Even though Cadet Moniac spent an extra year at the Academy in hopes of improving his class standing, he ranked thirty-ninth out of forty when he graduated on July 1, 1822. Then, after serving but a few months as a second lieutenant in the Sixth Infantry Regiment, Moniac resigned his commission because of family problems back home. His decision was probably also eased somewhat by the suggestion of President James Madison that officers not needed elsewhere should retire to civilian life where they could impart the benefits of their West Point training to the state militia. Moniac did enlist in the Alabama state militia as a private, but he had more success as a farmer raising cotton and breeding horses.

Ironically, even though he was married to a cousin of the Seminole leader Osceola, Moniac agreed in August 1836 to join the fight against his Seminole kinsmen as a captain in the Mounted Creek Volunteers. With the Second Seminole War going badly, the federal government promised the Muscogee volunteers for their service "the pay and emoluments and equipment of soldiers in the Army of the United States and such plunder as they may take from the Seminoles." Moniac was the only Native among the thirteen officers who commanded the regiment's 750 Creek volunteers. The Muscogees, who wore white turbans to distinguish themselves from their kinsmen, earned their money because the Seminoles were virtually unbeatable in their swampy homeland. After leading an attack against a strong Seminole encampment near Tampa in October, Moniac was promoted to major, but his budding military career ended abruptly a month later. Part of a combined force consisting of the Creek Volunteers, Tennessee Volunteers, and Florida militia, Moniac pressed the attack against a group of Seminole warriors hiding in a cypress swamp behind a stream connecting two lakes. When the Creek dragoons hesitated, fearing the narrow stream was too deep to wade across, Moniac lifted his sword and plunged forward.

The hidden Seminoles riddled him with thirteen musket balls. A witness to his death later wrote, "Major Moniac, an educated Creek warrior, in attempting to cross the creek, fell dead and the Seminoles were elated."

On Moniac's tombstone is engraved a quote by General Thomas Sydney Jesup, commander of all-US troops in the Second Seminole War: "David Moniac was as brave as any man who has drawn a sword and faced the enemy." Perhaps a more appropriate epitaph — one that would serve for most warriors in uniform — was written by historian Kenneth L. Benton: "He died as he lived, in two worlds: as a Major in the service of the United States Army — and as an Indian warrior in the service of his people."

Another prominent Indian soldier in this period was Ely S. Parker, a New York Seneca who fought for the North during the Civil War. Parker became General Ulysses S. Grant's secretary and achieved the rank of brevet brigadier general. After the war, he became the first Native American to head the Bureau of Indian Affairs, the government agency that has powerfully influenced the destiny of our nation's Native peoples since its establishment in 1824.

Parker was educated at a Baptist mission school and later studied law, but was denied admittance to the New York bar because, as an Indian, he was not an American citizen. He then studied civil engineering at Rensselaer Polytechnic Institute. When the Civil War broke out, Parker offered his services as an army engineer, but was refused a commission, again because of his Native heritage. Parker continued to press for a commission, becoming a captain of engineers in 1863. Because of an earlier friendship with General U. S. Grant, he was assigned to his staff and the following year became his secretary.

As in previous North American conflicts, the combatants welcomed Indians into their armies. Indeed, Native Americans fought fiercely for both sides in the war. As historian Laurence Hauptman points out in his important study *Between Two Fires*, many fought because they believed it was their last best hope to halt the wanton killing and expulsion of Native peoples that had begun on the East

General Ulysses S. Grant with his staff. Ely S. Parker is seated at far left. Courtesy National Archives and Records Administration.

Coast, continued through the "Trails of Tears" westward through the 1830s, and then exploded after the Gold Rush of 1849. But, as Hauptman points out, "the Civil War, rather than the last best hope, proved to be the final nail in the coffin in Indian efforts to stop the tide of American expansion."

As many as twenty thousand Native fighters contributed to Union or Confederate forces on both land and sea. They were present at most of the major battles and participated in the heaviest fighting of the war, including Second Bull Run, Antietam, the Wilderness, Spotsylvania, Cold Harbor, and the Union assaults on Petersburg. In fact, the last Confederate general to lay down his arms—two months after Lee—was Stand Watie, the Cherokee commander of the Indian regiments fighting in the western theater.

For the Confederacy, Native manpower was especially important, and Southern agents actively sought American Indian allies, especially among the Five Tribes—the Cherokee, Chickasaw, Choctaw, Muscogee (Creek), and Seminole. That these tribes joined the Confederacy was perhaps inevitable since the land they occupied adjoined Confederate states and many of their mixed-blood leaders were slaveholders sympathetic to the Southern cause. Moreover, the Confederate states offered them equal status in the Confederate government. The tribes could send representatives to the Confederate congress and had the right to tax merchants and traders within their boundaries. The Confederate government also promised the tribes compensation for damages caused by intruders during the war. As a result of Confederate inducements, the Five Tribes formally joined the Confederacy, and more than 15,000 uniformed Indian soldiers fought for the Southern cause, primarily in the western theater. Pea Ridge in Arkansas was their most significant battle. The Civil War divided the Five Tribes, however. Not all Natives in Indian Territory agreed with their leaders' Confederate sympathies, and some fought for the Union, while others spent the war as refugees.

Some 4,000 Indians fought for the North. Some served in the infantry; others were scouts and sharpshooters. The Indian volunteers wore their uniforms as proudly as their white comrades-in-arms, and they suffered the same horrendous casualty rates in this unbelievably brutal and bloody war. For example, of the 135 Oneida volunteers from Wisconsin who served in the Union Army, only 55 returned home, a mortality rate of nearly 60 percent.

Parker and a few other Native Americans received commissions in the Union Army and were recognized for their contributions to the war effort, but such cases were rare because many Union commanders regarded them as an enemy to be fought, not as warriors to be welcomed in their ranks. Besides concern about the reliability of Indian soldiers, some commanders worried they would revert to "savagery" on the battlefield. Warfare, as taught at West Point, was conducted according to prescribed rules and standards. As one Union officer reportedly said, "It is not the policy of our government to fight high-toned southern gentlemen with Indians."

Nonetheless, in the spring of 1862 the US secretary of war authorized the Department of the Missouri to enlist two or more Indian regiments for local service. Although these units would ostensibly be a "Home Guard," their unstated objective was the recovery of homes and lands lost to tribal members who had joined the Confederacy; therefore, it would involve Indians fighting Indians. Even this token gesture almost failed when the local Union commander refused to enlist Indians. The crisis was averted with the arrival of a new commandant, who ordered that the Indian regiments be formed as soon as possible.

The Indians performed so well that the War Department not only relaxed its objections to their use but even looked into making them eligible for the draft as the manpower demands of the Civil War mushroomed. The inquiry got no further than the US Department of the Interior, which pointed out that Indians were not citizens and thus could not be drafted.

The Anglo-American concern about the use of Indian soldiers appeared well founded, however, after scalped soldiers were found on the battlefields of Pea Ridge in March 1862 and Newtonia (in Missouri) the following September. These discoveries concerned both Union and Confederate commanders, who thereafter refrained from using Indian soldiers outside the Indian Territory.

Although the Indians made good soldiers, their lack of discipline did bother some white officers, but what could they expect from poorly trained recruits? Also disconcerting to white commanders was the Indian soldiers' general disdain for military virtues that were all important to professional officers, such as care of the uniform and proper military attitude. Self-approved furloughs and outright desertion were also common since the Native soldiers usually had little reason for their military service other than retrieving or protecting their homelands. The most striking example of this Native perspective was the desertion to the Union side by an entire regiment of Confederate Indians after the Home Guard captured the Cherokee capital of Tahlequah in Indian Territory.

Regardless what some officers may have thought about Indians in uniform, General Grant obviously valued the services of his aide Ely S. Parker. When Grant needed someone to draft a congratulatory letter to his army after its victory at Chattanooga, he gave the task to Parker because "he was good at that sort of thing." Later, at Appomattox Court House, Grant assigned him the task of transcribing the articles of surrender, because, as one of the Union officers admitted, Parker's "handwriting presented a better appearance than that of anyone else on the staff."

Robert E. Lee at first seemed somewhat taken aback at the dark-skinned Parker when Grant introduced the Confederate general to his staff. Perhaps he thought Grant was making a point by having a Black soldier present at the surrender ceremony before realizing that Parker was a Native American. "Well," Lee said while shaking Parker's hand, "I am glad to see one real American here." To which Parker replied, "Sir, we are all Americans."

Sources

Benton, Kenneth L. "Warrior from West Point." *Soldiers Magazine*, February 1974.

Hauptman, Laurence M. *Between Two Fires: American Indians in the Civil War*. Albuquerque: University of New Mexico Press, 1997.

Viola, Herman J. *After Columbus: The Smithsonian Chronicle of the North American Indians*. Washington, DC: Smithsonian Books, 1990.

Viola, Herman J. *The Indian Legacy of Charles Bird King*. Washington, DC: Smithsonian Institution Press, 1976.

Viola, Herman J. *Warriors in Uniform*. Washington, DC: National Geographic Society, 2008.

Warde, Mary Jane. *When the Wolf Came: The Civil War and the Indian Territory*. Fayetteville: University of Arkansas Press, 2013.

CHAPTER 2

Warriors of the West

Following the Civil War, the United States witnessed a dramatic increase in violence across the West as various Indian tribes lashed out at the tide of white settlement that poured across the Mississippi River after Appomattox. Faced with the realities of a shrinking army and a huge territory to patrol and pacify, military forces in the West increasingly came to recruit friendly Native Americans to help fight in their conflicts with the "hostiles." As a result, the concept of the Indian as the enemy slowly gave way to the realization that in western warfare the Indian could be an invaluable ally against other Indians. Recognizing this, Congress in 1866 authorized the army to enlist up to one thousand Indians "to act as scouts" and receive the pay and allowances of cavalry soldiers. This act formally opened the door for Native Americans to serve as enlisted personnel in the US Army.

For men who regarded warfare as honorable and horses and weapons as the tools of manhood, army service not only appealed to them but also enabled them to adjust to the white way of life on somewhat their own terms. Several tribes—notably the Tonkawa, the Warm Springs of Oregon, the Pawnee, the Wyoming Shoshone, and the Crow—maintained long-term relationships with the army.

For the Crow Nation, that relationship was dictated by the harsh realities of life on the northern plains after the Civil War as various tribes fought with one another as well as with white settlers over an ever-shrinking land base. The Crows' traditional homeland encompassed a vast area that stretched across much of present-day Wyoming and Montana. They were surrounded by several numerically superior and militant tribes, including the Lakota, the Cheyenne, and the Blackfeet. Constant warfare with these traditional enemies had made the Crows a brave and hardy people. It also helps explain why

Depiction of Custer's Last Stand at the Battle of the Little Bighorn, 1876. This highly dramatic and fanciful lithograph, titled *Custer's Last Fight*, established the popular image of the Battle of the Little Bighorn. Published in 1881 and distributed by the Anheuser Busch Company, it hung in saloons across America for decades. And it generated and reinforced false ideas about the conflict, such as Custer's long hair and saber—which he did not have—and the Native warriors' spears and shields, resembling the weapons of Zulu warriors rather than Plains Indians. The artist did visit the battlefield, so the terrain is somewhat accurate. Courtesy National Museum of American History, Smithsonian Institution.

they allied themselves with the US Army: its enemies—the Lakotas and Cheyennes—were also their enemies.

The violence on the northern plains escalated when the federal government opened a route in 1866 linking the Oregon Trail to the goldfields of Montana. Known as the Bozeman Trail, the road passed through pristine hunting grounds that belonged to the Crows but that were also coveted by Lakota tribal groups and the Cheyennes, who immediately attacked any white travelers they encountered. To protect those travelers, the US Army built a string of three forts along the trail—Phil Kearny, C. F. Smith, and Reno.

The posts had minimal garrisons and no Indian scouts, though fifty had been authorized. The Crows offered to provide 250 warriors to help protect the forts, but Commander Henry B. Carrington turned them down. He claimed he lacked both the authority to enlist them and the weapons needed to equip them. As a result, the posts endured months of siege conditions orchestrated by Red Cloud, the brilliant Oglala Lakota leader. Fort Phil Kearny, Carrington's headquarters, sustained more Indian attacks than any other post in US history, culminating in the destruction on December 6, 1866, of more than half its garrison in the Fetterman Fight. Crow Indian scouts doubtless would have alerted the garrison to the massive ambush that awaited Captain William J. Fetterman and his 81 troopers.

Although never given any official status, the Crows remained in the area of the Bozeman outposts until the army abandoned them in 1868. Had it not been for their presence, Fort C. F. Smith, which was even more isolated than Fort Phil Kearny, might have fared just as badly, but it was more centrally located in Crow country and the Lakotas and Cheyennes had no desire to tangle with them.

Having learned a bitter lesson along the Bozeman Trail, the army ten years later made ample use of Indian auxiliaries in the campaign to force Sitting Bull, Crazy Horse, and their defiant followers onto the Great Sioux Reservation. In the spring of 1876, the army sent three columns of troops to converge upon and trap the last free nomadic Indians, who were thought to be somewhere in the Bighorn country. One column, under General George Crook, marched northward from Fort Fetterman on the upper North Platte River. A second column, headed by Colonel John Gibbon, moved eastward from Fort Ellis in Montana. A third column, led by General Alfred Terry with the Seventh Cavalry, commanded by Lieutenant Colonel George Armstrong Custer, ventured west from Fort Lincoln in Dakota Territory.

Crook, who had successfully employed Apache soldiers to fight "hostile" Apaches, dispatched emissaries to the Crow Agency near Livingston, Montana, requesting the aid of Crow warriors in the campaign against the Lakotas and Cheyennes. The Crows authorized a force of 176 warriors led by chiefs Medicine Crow and Plenty Coups to join Crook, but as fighting allies and not merely as noncombatant scouts. With Crook were also some 200 Shoshones under the leadership of Chief Washakie.

Thanks to his Indian auxiliaries Crook was saved from the same fate that befell Custer a few days later. A large force of Lakotas and Cheyennes led by Crazy Horse almost caught the troopers by surprise as they prepared breakfast along the banks of the Rosebud River. Known as the Battle of the Rosebud, fought June 17, 1876, the fight was really between the Lakotas and Cheyennes on one side and the Crows and Shoshones on the other. According to the Indian combatants, the soldiers were just there and sometimes they were in the way. Although there were few casualties on either side, Crook's troopers expended so much ammunition in the six-hour fight that he retreated after Crazy Horse's followers returned to their camp along the Little Bighorn River.

Unaware of Crook's defeat, Terry and Gibbon met at the junction of the Rosebud and Yellowstone rivers without encountering any Indians. Upon receiving word that scouts had spotted a fresh trail heading toward the Little Bighorn, Terry sent Custer and the Seventh Cavalry south along the Rosebud in hopes of finding Sitting Bull's

Crow scout White Man Runs Him, photographed by Edward Curtis circa 1908. Courtesy Library of Congress.

camp. Once he found it, Custer was to block the Indian retreat into the Bighorn Mountains and await reinforcements.

With Custer were forty-seven Indian scouts—thirty-seven Arikaras, four Lakotas married to Arikara women, and six Crows. One of the Crow scouts was White Man Runs Him, whose nephew Joseph Medicine Crow was to earn his war honors as an infantryman fighting the Germans in World War II. Custer admired his Crow scouts, describing them in a letter to his wife, Libby, as "magnificent looking men, so much handsomer and more Indian-like than any we have ever seen, and so jolly and sportive; nothing of the gloomy, silent Redman about them." They had heard of Custer's toughness, that he never abandoned a trail and that, when his food ran out, he would eat mule. "That was the kind of man they wanted to fight under," Custer wrote; "they were willing to eat mule, too."

Custer may have admired his Crow scouts, but he failed to heed their advice. As White Man Runs Him later told his nephew, the Crow scouts succeeded in finding Sitting Bull's camp, but they also warned Custer that the enemy force was too large for the Seventh Cavalry to handle and advised him to await the promised reinforcements. Custer refused, lest Sitting Bull escape and deprive him of the victory he so desperately wanted and anticipated. Upon learning that Son of the Morning Star, the Crow name for Custer, planned an immediate attack, the scouts began removing their uniforms and putting on traditional fighting regalia.

"What are they doing?" Custer asked Mitch Bouyer, his chief of scouts. When Bouyer repeated the question to the scouts, one of them pointed his finger at Custer and said in Crow:

"Tell this man he's crazy! He is no good. Tell him that in a very short time we are all going to walk a path we never walked before. When we meet the Great Spirit, we want to be dressed as Crow warriors not as white men!"

Upon hearing this, Custer ordered the Crow scouts to leave. "I don't want that defeatist attitude around my soldiers," he told Bouyer. "We'll do the fighting if they are so afraid of the Sioux." That is why none of the Crow scouts died that day, though three Arikaras were killed, including Custer's favorite scout, Bloody Knife.

The disaster at Little Bighorn could have been averted if Custer had heeded the advice of his Crow scouts. In almost every other battle where the army used Indian scouts, the results were positive. The best example is provided by the Apache scouts who helped the US Army against their "hostile" kinsmen.

In 1871, as commander of the Arizona Territory at the time, George Crook was charged with subduing the Chiricahua Apaches, led by their indomitable leader Cochise, whose resistance to reservation life is not difficult to understand. As part of the federal government's Indian consolidation program, the Bureau of Indian Affairs assigned all the various Apache bands to San Carlos, a large reservation west of the Rio Grande along the Gila River. Of all the desolate pieces of landscape upon which the federal government placed Indians, San Carlos was one of the worst. "There was nothing but cactus, rattlesnakes, heat, rocks, and insects," recalled one of the Apaches who lived there. "No game, no edible plants. Many, many of our people died of starvation."

Believing that only an Apache could catch an Apache, Crook decided to recruit tribesmen from the San Carlos Reservation to join the fight, enlisting five companies of Chiricahua scouts—"the wildest I could get," he boasted. They were "wild" and they were tough. Within a year of the enlistment of the Apache scouts, Cochise and his followers surrendered and returned to San Carlos. In gratitude, Crook recommended that each of the ten Apache scouts who had a role in the successful campaign receive the Medal of Honor. "Without reserve or qualification of any nature," Crook wrote, "I assert that these scouts did excellent service, and were [of] more value in hunting down and compelling the surrender of the renegades than all the troops engaged in operations against them combined." Accordingly, on April 12, 1875, each scout received the medal "for gallant conduct during the campaigns and engagements with Apaches." For his part, Crook was appointed a brigadier general and sent to Fort Omaha in Nebraska to command the Department of the Platte.

THE MEDAL OF HONOR

The Medal of Honor was created by the US Congress in 1863 during the Civil War. Our nation's most prestigious military decoration, it is awarded to American military personnel who have distinguished themselves by acts of valor in combat. Thus far, twenty-nine warriors in uniform have received the medal, sixteen of them in the nineteenth century.

The first medal recipient was the Pawnee scout Sergeant Co-Tux-A-Kah-Wadde, or Traveling Bear, who was badly injured on July 8, 1869, when a fellow soldier shot him by mistake during an attack by the US Fifth Cavalry on a Cheyenne village camped along the Republican River in Kansas. Regrettably, the US Army misinterpreted his name as Co-Rux-Te-Chod-Ish (Mad Bear). That is the name on his Medal of Honor certificate, awarded August 24, 1869, and it remains Traveling Bear's incorrect name to this day.

Four Medal of Honor recipients were Mascogos or Black Seminoles. These were Africans who had escaped from slavery on southern plantations and joined the Seminoles in Florida. Eventually, the Black Seminoles and many of their Seminole allies left the United States and took up residence in Northern Mexico, where slavery was illegal. There the Black Seminoles worked for the Mexican government as military colonists defending the border from Apache and Comanche raiders. As they had in Florida, the Black Seminoles settled in their own villages, close to those of their Mexican allies. There they became known as Mascogos, a name evidently derived from the Muskogee or Creek people who were the ancestors of the Seminoles.

After slavery was abolished in the United States following the Civil War, many of the Black Seminoles left Mexico and took up residence in Texas. Known for their bravery and military prowess, Black Seminoles enlisted in the US Army as scouts in the continuing conflicts with Apache and Comanche raiders. The official name of the unit, formed in 1870 and disbanded in 1914 was the Seminole Negro Indian Scouts. In one noted engagement, Lieutenant John L. Bullis, the officer in command of the Black Seminole scouts, accompanied by three of them, encountered a Comanche war party. Greatly outnumbered, Bullis and his scouts left the safety of the rocks in which they were hiding and rushed to mount their horses. The three scouts made it safely, but Bullis was bucked off his horse. When the scouts saw he had been left behind and was surrounded by Comanche warriors, they rushed back to rescue him. As Scout John Ward pulled Bullis up behind him on his horse, the other two scouts—trumpeter Isaac Payne and Private Pompey Factor—provided covering fire to keep the Comanches at bay. Then, the four soldiers, riding on three horses, managed to escape. As Lieutenant Bullis later reported, the three Black Seminoles had "saved my hair." For their "bravery and trustworthiness" each of them received the Medal of Honor.

The last Medal of Honor awarded to an Indian soldier in the nineteenth century went to Yavapai scout Yuma William Rowdy. He received his medal on May 15, 1890, for heroism in the final conflict with renegade Apaches during the Cherry Creek campaign in Arizona Territory.

The tranquility in the Southwest was short-lived. Various Apache leaders resented reservation life and left the reservation, continuing regional turmoil for more than a decade. The most determined renegade was Geronimo. Unhappy with the settled life the US government was imposing on his people, he left San Carlos in August 1881 with some one hundred men, women, and children. A few months later he returned, killed the San Carlos police chief, and forced several hundred Chiricahuas to join him in Mexico. The result was another Apache war that kept the Southwest in turmoil for the next five years. Determined to restore order, the US Army reassigned General Crook to the region, and he, once again, turned to the Apache scouts for assistance.

Among the scouts who answered his call was Sergeant William Alchesay, one of the ten Apache Medal of Honor recipients and a friend of Geronimo. On March 27, 1886, Alchesay met with Geronimo in his camp at Canyon de los Embudos in Sonora, Mexico, and

Congressional Medal of Honor recipient Scout William Alchesay (Apache; 1853–1928), who later became chief of the White Mountain Apaches. Courtesy National Archives and Records Administration.

persuaded him to return to the San Carlos Reservation. As Alchesay informed Crook after meeting with Geronimo, "They have all surrendered. There is nothing more to be done. I don't want you [to] have any bad feelings about the Chiricahuas. I am glad they have surrendered because they are all one family with me." Although Geronimo changed his mind and slipped away with a few of his warriors, his freedom was short-lived and he surrendered for good a few months later. Nonetheless, he and Alchesay remained close friends until Geronimo's death in 1909.

Alchesay, who served more than fourteen years in the US Army, eventually became a chief of the White Mountain Apache Tribe. Before his death in 1928, he made several trips to Washington, DC, to visit with President Grover Cleveland on tribal business. He also provided service as a counselor to Indian agents in Arizona Territory. In recognition of his life of selfless public service, the US Army in 1975 named Alchesay Barracks at Fort Huachuca, Arizona, in his honor and in 2012 inducted him into the Military Intelligence Hall of Fame.

A sad footnote to the role of the Apache scouts is that many of them—but not Alchesay—suffered the same fate as their "renegade" relatives. The government sent some five hundred Chiricahua Apaches to detention camps in Florida, Alabama, and Oklahoma, where they remained for decades. Considering it an act of betrayal, General Crook, who died in 1890, spent the rest of his life working for the return of the Apaches to their Arizona homeland, which did not occur until 1913.

Following the Wounded Knee Massacre in December 1890, the army tried the experiment of enlisting Indians not as short-term scouts but as soldiers serving five-year tours of duty in regular units. The idea was to help the Indians assimilate into mainstream American society while earning an income.

The program at first enjoyed remarkable success. The new recruits excelled in all facets of military deportment. An Apache company organized at Mount Vernon Barracks in Alabama from former prisoners of war, proved so efficient at drill that the regimental commander placed it in the honored position of "advanced guard" in battalion demonstrations. The Apache soldiers relished every opportunity to wear dress uniforms and demonstrate their abilities on the parade ground. Their commanding officer judged their intelligence to be far superior to that of the local citizens, especially the so-called "sand hill tackies" who hovered around the base ridiculing the Apache soldiers.

After that initial success, however, recruitment among reservation Indians faltered badly. Despite extensive efforts to attract recruits from eastern Indian schools, by the summer of 1895, the 1,000 Indian soldiers had dwindled to 67 men at Fort Sill, Oklahoma. This was Troop L of the Seventh Cavalry, commanded by Captain Hugh Lenox Scott. After two years passed and no Indians had enlisted, the army declared the experiment a failure and discharged Troop L on May 31, 1897.

Why did the experiment fail? It was not the discipline or drill the Indian soldiers disliked; they could handle whatever the army handed them. They objected to a system that violated cultural values such as making them cut their hair and living in framed buildings. They did not like the long-term enlistments or being stationed far away from their families. They also disliked much of the manual labor, which they called "women's work."

On the part of the army, however, the core of the problem may have been latent racism. General O. O. Howard, the famed Civil War general and founder of Howard University, the historically Black college in Washington, DC, said the experiment had been doomed from its inception because of the fear that one day white soldiers would have to take orders from Indian noncommissioned officers. Twenty years after his troop of Indian soldiers had been discharged, Hugh Scott, now a general in the US Army, confided to a friend that the Indian soldiers had been cheated of their success by an air of prejudice in the War Department.

Certainly, not all army officers welcomed Indians into their ranks. Some expressed concern about employing Indians as soldiers, claiming they did not have "the patriotic instincts a soldier must have," even though some Native soldiers charged up San Juan Hill with Theodore Roosevelt's "Rough Riders" during the Spanish-American War, others fought in the Philippines, and a few saw action in China during the Boxer Rebellion. Not until the outbreak of the First World War was there a real change in attitude about Indians serving in the US armed forces.

Sources

Dunlay, Thomas W. *Wolves for the Blue Soldiers: Indian Scouts and Auxiliaries with the United States Army, 1860–90*. Lincoln: University of Nebraska Press, 1982.

Monnett, John H., ed. *Eyewitness to the Fetterman Fight: Indian Views*. Norman: University of Oklahoma Press, 2017.

Mulroy, Kevin. *The Seminole Freedmen: A History.* Norman: University of Oklahoma Press, 2007.

"Native American Medal of Honor Recipients." U.S. Army Center of Military History. Accessed June 9, 2021. https://history.army.mil/html/topics/natam/natam-moh.html.

Porter, Kenneth W. *The Black Seminoles: History of a Freedom-Seeking People.* Revised and edited by Alcione M. Amos and Thomas P. Senter. Gainesville: University Press of Florida, 1996.

Viola, Herman J. *Little Bighorn Remembered: The Untold Indian Story of Custer's Last Stand.* New York: Times Books, 1999.

White, William B. "The Military and the Melting Pot: The American Army and Minority Groups, 1865–1894." Ph.D. dissertation, University of Wisconsin, 1968.

CHAPTER 3

World War I

Doughboys Devise a Code

World War I, also known as the Great War, was one of the most horrific conflicts ever known. Begun in 1914, it pitted the countries of Germany, Austria-Hungary, and Turkey, known as the Central Powers, against Great Britain, France, Italy, Russia, and later the United States, known as the Allies, and it witnessed the use of weapons never before seen in combat, such as tanks, poison gas, flame throwers, and airplanes. By 1917 when the United States entered the conflict on the Allied side, more than five million soldiers had already been killed or wounded with no end in sight as both sides faced each other from trenches that stretched in a four-hundred-mile line called the Western Front. Sometimes only a few hundred yards apart, the opposing trenches ran from the North Sea, through France and Belgium, to the Alps.

The trenches, usually about four feet wide and eight feet deep with some places much shallower, were reinforced with sandbags, logs, or sheet metal. All along both sets of trenches were strong points, sometimes built of concrete, with machine guns, as well as short trenches that extended about thirty feet toward the enemy line where sentries could listen for enemy troops attempting to sneak up at night. And all across the Western Front was an area known as No-Man's-Land, the space between the fifty or so feet of barbed-wire entanglements that protected both trenches.

No matter how realistic their training was, nothing could have prepared the Americans for the horrors of the Western Front. Shellfire and trenches after four years of conflict had left the battlefields so churned up that they looked like the surface of the moon, and poison gas had killed much of the vegetation. Because the trenches were often knee-deep in water after it rained, a wounded soldier might drown in the mud. In fact, the two most repulsive memories of life in the trenches were rats and the bodies of dead soldiers. Rats were everywhere, feeding on food scraps and the bodies of dead soldiers, who were often buried in or near the trenches where artillery blasts would dig them up.

This was the situation the American troops faced when they arrived on the Western Front in the summer of 1917. Anxious to bring the war to a close and now bolstered by the energy and enthusiasm of thousands of US soldiers, the Allies hoped to launch a series of surprise attacks across the No-Man's-Land and drive the Germans from their trenches. Essential to the success of the surprise attacks, however, was secrecy. Battles are won and lost on the ability to communicate secretly. It has always been a matter of life and death.

Before the Americans arrived, the Allies had tried a variety of communication systems such as runners, pigeons, dogs, the telegraph, telephones, and wireless radios to send messages while fighting and to keep rear-echelon commanders in touch with their frontline troops, but each had drawbacks.

Runners probably had the most dangerous jobs in the war because they had to leave the relative safety of the trenches, cross open ground, and be exposed to enemy fire, which meant death or capture. In fact, the Germans killed or captured one in four of the Allied runners.

Carrier pigeons were another means of communication. At the start of the war the British had 60 pigeons and 15 handlers in the warzone. By 1918 there were more than 20,000 pigeons and 370 handlers. Pigeons could fly over 100 miles at an average speed of 50 miles per hour. When a bird returned to its home loft, it would trigger a wire that rang a bell, alerting the handler. But pigeons were easily spotted and shot.

One of the avian heroes of World War I was a carrier pigeon named Cher Ami. On October 3, 1918, some 200 soldiers found themselves surrounded by German soldiers behind enemy lines where they were

Cher Ami. War
Department. U.S.
Signal Corps. Courtesy
National Museum of
American History.

trapped for five days. During this time they were receiving friendly
fire from the Allies, who did not know Americans were in the midst of
the Germans. The only way they could inform the Allies of their pre-
dicament was by pigeon, and several were sent. Two were shot down
and a third had the wrong coordinates. Their situation now desper-
ate, the trapped soldiers dispatched Cher Ami, their last pigeon. On
her left leg she carried a small canister with this message written on
onionskin: "We are along the road parallel to 276.4. Our own artillery
is dropping a barrage directly on us. For heavens sake stop it."

As Cher Ami took off, the Germans opened fire and she fell to the
ground. Somehow, after only a few seconds, she managed to take
flight again and arrived at her home loft twenty-five miles to the rear
a half hour later, thereby saving the lives of the 194 survivors. She
had been shot through the breast, was blinded in one eye, and had
a leg hanging by only a tendon. Army medics managed to save her
life, but were unable to repair her leg, so they carved a small one out
of wood. For her heroism, the French government awarded her the

Croix de Guerre medal with a palm Oak Leaf Cluster. After she died in 1919, Cher Ami was given to the Smithsonian Institution, where she is on display in the National Museum of American History.

Dogs were also used to carry messages, and some 20,000 canines served during the war. Most were family pets donated to the war effort or strays taken from pounds. Dogs were sent out when conditions were considered too dangerous for human messengers. Fast and low to the ground, they were less likely to be shot than runners and could cross most forms of terrain. Trained to return one-way to their keeper's station, dogs could cover ten to fifteen miles in one to two hours, but their companionship was so highly valued in the trenches that soldiers would often offer to deliver messages in their place.

A canine hero of World War I was Sergeant Stubby, a brindle dog with a short tail. Private James Robert Conroy found Stubby while training at Yale University and smuggled him to France, where he

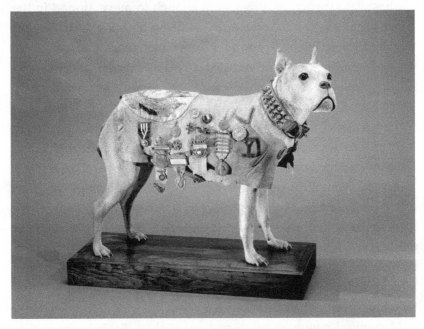

Sergeant Stubby. Photo by J. Robert Conroy. Courtesy
National Museum of American History.

became the mascot of the 102nd Infantry, 26th Yankee Division. Stubby learned bugle calls and drills and could even salute by putting his right paw on his right eyebrow.

Stubby quickly adjusted to combat and earned a remarkable war record. After recovering from gas exposure, he was able to detect the tiniest trace of gas. One morning, while most of the soldiers in his unit were sleeping, he smelled gas and alerted them by barking and running through the trench. He also located wounded men lying in No-Man's-Land, barking until paramedics arrived, and he would lead lost soldiers back to their trenches. Once he surprised a German soldier drawing a map of the trenches and began to bark. When the German ran, Stubby knocked him down and held him prisoner until American soldiers arrived and captured the spy. For this exploit he was given the rank of sergeant, thereby becoming the first dog to be given a rank in the armed forces of the United States. Later, Stubby was injured during a grenade attack and sent to a Red Cross recovery hospital for surgery. When well enough to move around in the hospital, he would visit wounded soldiers, boosting their morale. By the end of the war, Stubby had served in seventeen battles. After the war he met Presidents Woodrow Wilson, Warren Harding, and Calvin Coolidge and received numerous medals for his heroism. When Private Conroy began studying law at Georgetown University, Stubby became the mascot of the Georgetown Hoyas. After he died in 1926, Stubby was mounted and given to the Smithsonian's National Museum of American History, where he joined Cher Ami on display.

Another communication method was visual signaling with flags or lamps. Based on Morse code, the system required a trained signaler and a trained receiver with a telescope, pencil, and notepad at either end. This form of communication was quicker and safer than using runners, but the effective distances were relatively short. And it had a serious drawback: both signaling units were easily spotted, thereby exposing their positions to enemy fire.

Mechanical communication systems such as the telegraph, telephone, and wireless radio were available, but each also had drawbacks.

The telephone and telegraph were effective at sending messages over long distances, but they required the use of wires, and when the fighting started, they were all too easily cut or disconnected. Moreover, the Germans were adept at intercepting and decoding their messages.

The wireless radio, patented by Guglielmo Marconi in 1896, was still in its infancy when the war began. Although used extensively, the transmitter and receiver were not only heavy and fragile but also extremely vulnerable to enemy interception, thus requiring elaborate codes that considerably hindered its use.

No matter how elaborate the codes, however, the Germans managed to intercept and decode almost every message the Allies sent, making it impossible to execute maneuvers requiring stealth and surprise. As a result, surprise attacks seldom succeeded, and thus both sides remained entrenched month after month, year after year, while inflicting horrendous casualties on each other from artillery barrages, fruitless frontal assaults, poison gas attacks, and disease.

All this changed once the United States entered the war, thanks to the fact that thousands of Native Americans volunteered to join the fight. Although most Native men in 1917 were not liable to the draft because they were not US citizens, they enlisted in astonishing numbers. The Bureau of Indian Affairs later declared that of the 10,000 Native Americans who served in the army and the 2,000 who served in the US Navy, fully three out of four were volunteers. Several tribes even made it "their" war. Most notable was the Onondaga Nation of the once-feared Iroquois Confederacy. It unilaterally declared war on Germany, citing the ill-treatment accorded tribal members performing with a Wild West show who were stranded in Berlin when hostilities began. A few weeks later the Oneida Nation, another member of the Iroquois Confederacy, followed with its own declaration of war.

The Great War proved a watershed for America's Native peoples, who established a remarkable record of patriotism and heroism in a conflict for which they had no readily apparent reason to join or recognize. The first decorated war hero from South Dakota, for example, was Chauncey Eagle-Horn, who was killed in France. His father had fought Custer at the Battle of the Little Bighorn. Joe Young Hawk, the son of one of Custer's Arikara scouts at the battle, was wounded and taken prisoner by the Germans but later escaped after killing three of his guards and capturing two others.

The greatest contribution the Indian doughboys made to the war effort—a contribution largely unrecognized at the time—was not their battlefield heroism but their linguistic abilities. Indeed, their Native languages turned out to be an unexpected benefit of assigning the uniformed warriors to serve as messengers and telephone operators. The Germans were unable to understand their languages. In the US Army's 36th Division alone, which consisted of soldiers from Texas and Oklahoma, were nearly one thousand Indians from twenty-six tribes speaking different languages or dialects, none of which the Germans could either understand or translate. A captured German later admitted that they could not make any sense of the Indian messages that they intercepted. "What language were they speaking?" he asked. "American," his captors told him.

Organized as regular infantry and given training at Camp Bowie near Fort Worth, Texas, the first unit of the 36th Division transferred to France in May 19, 1918; the last arrived in August of that year. On October 6, the regiment moved to the Western Front, and it was there the decision was made to use Indians to send messages, a decision that occurred evidently by accident. A captain overheard two Choctaw soldiers, Solomon Louis and Mitchell Bobb, talking to each other in their native language. Even though he had heard it many times, he could not understand what they were saying. Suddenly, a light went on: "This is our code," he thought—"it's unbreakable."

The captain sent his idea to regimental headquarters, where it was immediately acted upon by posting Choctaw speakers in the headquarters of each field company to deliver military communications via field telephone and translate radio messages into their language. As Colonel A. W. Bloor, commander of the 142nd Infantry, later informed his superiors, "There was hardly one chance in a million that Fritz

[Germans soldiers] would be able to translate these dialects, and the plan to have these Indians transmit telephone messages was adopted."

The first use of the Choctaw speakers was made in withdrawing two companies of the 2nd Battalion from the front during the night of October 26. Because the movement was completed without mishap, the Choctaws were used the next day in the successful assault on a strongly fortified German position called Forest Ferme. "The enemy's complete surprise is evidence that he could not decipher the messages," Colonel Bloor was pleased to report.

Germany surrendered on November 11, 1918, less than three weeks after the Indian doughboys began sending their messages. How much credit the Indians deserve for the Allied victory is hard to determine, but their service certainly played a key role in that triumph.

Nineteen Choctaw doughboys earned immortality as the first "Code Talkers." Ranging in age from nineteen to thirty-five, they were Albert Billy, Mitchell Bobb, Victor Brown, Ben Carterby, Benjamin Colbert, George Davenport, Joseph Davenport, James M. Edwards, Tobias William Frazier, Benjamin W. Hampton, Noel Johnson, Otis Leader, Solomon Bond Louis, Peter Maytubby, Joseph Oklahombi, Jeff Nelson, Robert Taylor, Walter Veach, and Calvin Wilson.

One difficulty posed by this novel arrangement—a precursor of the better-organized and more widely known Navajo code program of World War II—was the lack of military words in the Indian vocabulary. No matter. The Choctaws devised a workable code: for a cannon the Choctaw soldiers used their term for "big gun"; a "little gun shoots fast" was a machine gun, a "tribe" was a regiment, a "grain of corn" was a battalion, a "stone" was a hand grenade; poison gas was "bad air," casualties were "scalps," tanks were "turtles," and a patrol was "many scouts."

Although the Choctaws are credited as being the first Code Talkers, other Indian doughboys are known to have communicated with one another in their native languages on the battlefield, including Cheyennes, Comanches, Osages, and Lakotas. The great irony, of

Members of the Choctaw Telephone Squad, 1917–1918, who sent messages in their language during World War I, blazing the trail for the Code Talkers of World War II. *Left to right:* Solomon Louis, Mitchell Bobb, James Edwards, Calvin Wilson, James Davenport, and Captain E. H. Horner. Courtesy Wanamaker Collection, Indiana University.

course, is that while the tribal soldiers were honored for the use of their languages on the Western Front, Indian children at home were being punished when they spoke in their native tongues at school.

Little was ever said or written about the role of the Choctaw Code Talkers after the war. In fact, the Choctaw veterans never referred to themselves as "code talkers," and the phrase was not coined until years later. One of the Choctaws, Tobias Frazier, called what they did "talking on the radio." Nonetheless, the tribal speakers in the Great War blazed the trail for those who followed their lead as Code Talkers in World War II.

OTIS W. LEADER

One of the World War I Choctaw Code Talkers was Otis W. Leader. On April 5, 1917, secret service agents spotted Otis with two Swiss companions in the Fort Worth, Texas, stockyards and confronted them. The agents suspected them of being German spies because of their accents. The following day the United States declared war on Germany, and a week later the thirty-five-year-old Choctaw, still angry at the unfair accusation, enlisted in the army. By June, he was in France.

Because Leader and his unit, the 1st Division, were the first American combat troops to arrive in France, they were invited to march in a July Fourth parade in Paris. At that parade a French artist, Raymond Desvarreux, carried a commission from the French government and a letter granting permission signed by General John J. Pershing, the

Portrait of Choctaw soldier Otis Leader painted in 1917 by the French artist Raymond Desvarreaux-Larpenteur. Musée de l'Armée, Dist. RMN-Grand Palais / Art Resource, NY.

commander of the American Expeditionary Force, to paint the ideal US soldier. The soldier he selected was Leader. As Desvarreux later explained, he chose the Choctaw Indian from Oklahoma because he was "straight as an arrow and standing over six feet tall; keen, alert, yet with calmness that betokens strength and his naturally bronzed face reflecting the spirit that . . . [the Americans] took across with them, the spirit that eventually turned the tide."

The artist did not exaggerate. General Pershing later called Leader "the war's greatest fighting machine," and a fighting machine he was. According to news accounts, in heavy fighting at Chateau-Thierry on July 18, 1918, Leader's machine gun company received some of the very first German fire to hit American soldiers. When three of the four men in his machine gun crew were killed, Leader grabbed a rifle, rushed toward the Germans, and captured eighteen.

Leader, who rose to the rank of sergeant, was wounded twice and gassed three times. At the war's end he was in a French hospital recovering from shrapnel wounds. For his valor, Leader received a Purple Heart, two Silver Stars, the Distinguished Service Cross, nine battle stars, and two individual awards of the Croix de Guerre, a French military honor established during World War I.

JOSEPH OKLAHOMBI

Another Choctaw hero was Private Joseph Oklahombi. His name means "People Killer" in the Choctaw language. While on patrol the evening of October 8, 1918, Joseph and twenty-three fellow soldiers encountered a large and heavily armed German force near Saint-Étienne-à-Arnes. At one point in the ensuing battle, Joseph managed to work his way through some 200 yards of barbed-wire entanglements in No-Man's-Land and seize one of the enemy machine guns, which he then turned on the much larger German force. He and his companions held their position for four days despite fierce counterattacks. Joseph crossed over the open terrain several times, delivering coded messages and helping tend to his wounded comrades. Unable to dislodge the Americans after four days of combat, the Germans finally surrendered. All told, Oklahombi and his comrades killed 79 Germans and captured 171. In recognition of his bravery, the French government gave him the Croix de Guerre with Palm, one of the country's highest military awards. He later received the Silver Star from the United States.

Choctaw Code Talker Joseph Oklahombi. Courtesy Oklahoma Historical Society.

Sources

Britten, Thomas A. *American Indians in World War I: At War and at Home.* Albuquerque: University of New Mexco Press, 1997.

Meadows, William C. *The First Code Talkers: Native American Communicators in World War I.* Norman: University of Oklahoma Press, 2021.

Phillips, Mary. "French Artist Picked Outstanding Oklahoman as Subject of War Painting." *Oklahoman,* August 17, 2010.

Viola, Herman J. *Warriors in Uniform.* Washington, DC: National Geographic Society, 2008.

CHAPTER 4

World War II

Warrior Spirit Rises

At least 5,000 Indians were in uniform in the US Army, Navy, Air Force, Coast Guard, and National Guard prior to the Japanese attack on Pearl Harbor on December 7, 1941. Upon the US declaration of war thousands more immediately rushed to enlist. Half the eligible males on some reservations volunteered for duty. By 1942, at least 99 percent of all eligible Indian males had registered for the draft. Had all eligible non-Indian males in the United States enlisted in the same proportion as did tribal people, there would have been no need for the Selective Service System.

The Bureau of Indian Affairs later reported that 24,521 reservation Indians saw military service during the war. About 20,000 nonreservation Indians also served. In other words, something like 45,000 Indians, more than 10 percent of the entire estimated Native American population of 350,000 in the United States at the time, saw active duty in the armed forces during World War II. This represented one-third of all able-bodied Native men from 18 to 50 years of age. In some tribes, the percentage of men in the military reached as high as 70 percent. In addition, several hundred Indian women served in the WAC, WAVES, and Army Nurse Corps.

A common misunderstanding among the Indian volunteers was the expectation that everyone who registered for the draft would be called into service. Not so. Many were turned down for age or health reasons. "I rejected seven times on account of having old," a Pima man complained. "I am only 37 years old." Another Arizona Indian, rejected for being overweight, argued: "Don't want to run. Want to

The second flag raising on Mount Suribachi, Iwo Jima, February 23, 1945, photographed by Joe Rosenthal. Courtesy National Museum of the American Indian, Smithsonian Institution.

fight." A Chippewa (Ojibwe) man, rejected because he had no teeth, snapped: "I don't want to bite 'em. I just want to shoot 'em!"

All told, counting the American Indians who worked in the defense industry as well as those who joined the armed forces, about 20 percent of the Native population, or 80,000 men and women, joined the fight against Adolph Hitler, a man they called "He Who Smells His Moustache," and Benito Mussolini, whom they dubbed "Gourd Chin." American Indians also invested more than $50 million in war bonds and contributed generously to the Red Cross and the Army and Navy Relief societies. It was a remarkable show of loyalty on the part of a people who had lost almost all but their pride, dignity, and warrior spirit at the hands of the federal government.

Among the thousands of Native Americans who served in World War II, two deserve special recognition for their shared exploits atop Mount Suribachi during the battle to capture Iwo Jima, the Japanese stronghold in the South Pacific. Iwo Jima, one of the Japanese home islands, witnessed some of the fiercest fighting in the Pacific campaign. When the battle began on February 19, 1945, 22,000 Japanese occupied the island. At its end, thirty-five days later, the only known Japanese survivors were 216 prisoners of war. But the Americans paid dearly for their victory, suffering more than 26,000 casualties, including 6,800 dead.

The two Indians who deserve recognition for their roles on Iwo Jima were both Marines. One—Ira Hamilton Hayes—was applauded as a hero and achieved fame and notoriety; the other—Louis Charles Charlo, a true hero, became lost to history.

Ira Hayes is undoubtedly the best-known Indian who served in World War II, thanks to the celebrated photograph that combat photographer Joe Rosenthal took of Ira and five other soldiers raising the US flag atop Mount Suribachi. Three of the flag raisers died in the continued fighting.

Rosenthal's photograph captured the American imagination. Hoping to capitalize on that dramatic moment, President Harry Truman

Ira Hayes attended the US Marine Corps parachutist school in San Diego, where he was dubbed "Chief Falling Cloud." Courtesy National Museum of the American Indian.

summoned Ira back to the United States to aid a war bond drive. Although acclaimed a hero, Ira felt he had done nothing heroic. "How could I feel like a hero," he lamented, "when only five men in my platoon of 45 survived, when only 27 men in my company of 250 managed to escape death or injury?" Instead of being shuttled from city to city for publicity purposes, Ira simply wanted to return to the war. "Sometimes I wish that guy had never made that picture," he confessed. After the war, Ira attempted to lead an anonymous life on the Pima reservation, but it was impossible. Suffering from PTSD (though not recognized as a medical condition at the time), Hayes could find escape from his pain only through alcohol. Never married, unable to get his life back in balance, he died of exposure in January 1955 at the age of thirty-three, just ten weeks after attending the dedication ceremony at Arlington National Cemetery in Washington, DC, for the Iwo Jima Memorial, the bronze cast replica of the photograph that had caused him so much torment.

In truth, the stirring Rosenthal photograph documents what was the second flag raising atop Mount Suribachi on February 23, 1945. Marine private Louis Charlo, a member of the Bitterroot Salish Tribe of Montana, had a key part in the first flag raising.

Private First Class Louis Charles Charlo, a member of the Bitterroot Salish Nation, was born in Missoula, Montana. By a remarkable coincidence, the ship that carried him to Iwo Jima was the USS *Missoula*. Courtesy Victor Charlo.

On February 23, the fourth day of the Iwo Jima campaign, the Marines sent two patrols to the summit of 546-foot-high Mount Suribachi in an effort to determine how many Japanese still held out in the island's maze of caves and tunnels. Private Charlo, a BAR (Browning Automatic Rifle) man with F Company of the 28th Regiment, 5th Marine Division, accompanied one of the patrols. After encountering no resistance, his patrol returned to the command center and then led a group of about 40 Marines back up the mountain, where a 20-foot piece of pipe was found. To it they lashed a flag taken from the USS *Missoula*. As they raised the flag, Louis R. Lowery of *Leatherneck* magazine snapped a photograph. According to the official Marine Corps account of this first flag raising, Louis Charlo was one of the men in the photo. Decades later, another Marine disputed the claim and the Marine Corps accepted the challenge. Nonetheless,

Private Charlo *(in foreground, facing the camera)*, photographed by Marine Corps sergeant Louis R. Burmeister after the first flag raising on Mount Suribachi, February 23, 1945. Courtesy US Marine Corps.

as other photos of the event document, Private Charlo was with the first flag raisers.

On March 2, less than a week later, Private Charlo, age nineteen, was killed attempting to rescue Private Ed McLaughlin, a wounded comrade stranded in an area of the Iwo Jima battlefield known as the Meat Grinder. According to his platoon leader, "Chuck" was carrying McLaughlin on his back when Japanese snipers killed them both just a few feet from safety.

Although Charlo deserved a medal for heroism, the only award his family received was his Purple Heart. According to General Robert Neller, commandant of the Marine Corps, writing on August 21, 2016, "There is no record of any medal being submitted or awarded ... [but] I can't emphasize enough that our Corps considers him a hero. He was part of one of the most brutal battles of World War II and gave everything for his Corps and country."

The US government's failure to recognize Charlo with a medal was not unusual for Native American servicemen and women. For example, of the 464 soldiers awarded the Congressional Medal of Honor—"for gallantry above and beyond the call of duty"—during World War II, only 5 went to Native Americans: navy commander Ernest Evans, Cherokee; Private First Class John Reese Jr., Cherokee; Lieutenant Jack C. Montgomery, Cherokee; Lieutenant Ernest Childers, Muscogee (Creek); and Lieutenant Van Barfoot, Choctaw.

Of the known American Indians in the various branches of the armed forces during World War II, 550 were killed—the first one died at Pearl Harbor—and more than 700 were wounded. To those warriors in uniform, the United States awarded 71 Air Medals, 34 Distinguished Flying Crosses, 51 Silver Stars, 47 Bronze Stars, and the 5 Medals of Honor.

Three of the Medal of Honor recipients—Montgomery, Childers, and Barfoot—served in the same unit, the 45th Division. Known as the Fighting 45th, the division was a reserve unit from Oklahoma, New Mexico, and Arizona, and many of its troops—600 from some 50 different tribes—were Native Americans. The unit's distinctive

Sergeant Brummett Echohawk (1922–2006), the Pawnee artist who perfected his talent on the battlefields of Italy and later became one of Oklahoma's best-known artists after World War II. Courtesy of Joel Echohawk.

patch bore a gold thunderbird on a red background in tribute to its Native personnel.

One of the Indian soldiers in the Fighting 45th was Brummett Echohawk, a Pawnee who earned three Purple Hearts and three Bronze Stars for his exploits in Italy during World War II. After the war, he became one of Oklahoma's best-known artists, a talent he had perfected during lulls on the battlefield.

Brummett began sketching the war while in Sicily. "On about the first day," he wrote in his memoirs, published as *Drawing Fire*, "I found drawing paper and pencils in a battered enemy garrison. From that day forward, I sketched the war. I used the back of a mess kit lid as a drawing board. I did not show off my drawings, for we were all sick of seeing the dead, bloated bodies in the hot Sicilian sun. Most of the sketching was done during a lull, or when in Battalion reserve. I carried my drawing paper in an empty 60 MM waterproof carton. The small tubular carton fit snugly in my combat pack." When drawing soldiers, he frequently made two sketches, one for his model and one for himself. He even gave copies to German prisoners whom he sketched.

Brummett's drawings became public—and his career as an artist was launched—while recuperating from injuries in an army hospital where a war correspondent discovered them. As a result, the Newspaper Enterprise Association bought several of his drawings and distributed them to its client newspapers in the States. The army weekly newsletter *Yank* also published some of his work. Because constant fighting left little time for drawing, he later joked, "I became the fastest pen in the West."

But, as Brummett reveals in his memoirs, when he dropped out of high school in 1940 at age seventeen and joined the National Guard, he aspired to be a warrior, not an artist. "When I was young, growing up in Pawnee, Oklahoma," he wrote, "I used to listen to old-time Pawnee Indians tell stories of warriors and battles on the Great Plains. When a warrior distinguished himself in battle, the people gave him a name with great ceremony. The name was one of honor. Songs were composed describing his feats of bravery. Kept as history, the songs were handed down from generation to generation. The warrior was held in honor all his life because he had defended his people and country. My grandfather had been a great warrior. He died when I was two years old; however, I got to see other old Pawnee warriors. In their twilight years, they still carried themselves proud. Seeing them and respecting them, I wanted very much to be a warrior myself."

As a sergeant in Company B of the 179th Regimental Combat Team, an all-Indian unit from Pawnee, Brummett fulfilled his dream. He was part of the American force that landed in Sicily and then stormed ashore at Anzio.

Although Anzio proved a turning point in the victory of the Allies in World War II, for Brummett, it was "a night mare—a complete night mare." It also ended his military career. "With leg and foot wounds and having taken concussion hits that left me with internal injuries and a partial loss of hearing, I was furloughed home to Pawnee, Oklahoma." There he met Phillip Gover, his platoon sergeant, who had lost an arm. Also there from his platoon was Sergeant Floyd Good Buffalo Rice, who had suffered a wound in the

*Sgt. Phillip Gover—
Pawnee Thunderbird,*
painting by Brummett
Echohawk. Courtesy of
Joel EchoHawk and the
45th Infantry Division
Museum, Oklahoma City.

temple and ear. While the three soldiers were home together, the Pawnee tribe honored them "as true warriors." A song was composed for them and each was awarded a warrior's name.

Most of the American Indians who fought, were wounded, or died on the far-flung battlefields of World War II were nameless and forgotten to the vast majority of Americans, but not to their fellow tribespeople, who honored the tribe's soldiers for their military service and often revered them afterward.

One of the warrior heroes unsung by the American majority was Andrew Bird-in-Ground. During the Allied landing in Normandy, he earned the Bronze Star with three clusters. His people, the Crows, felt he would have received the Medal of Honor but for the fact that he was an Indian. When Andrew returned from the war, he was given a new name, Kills Many Germans, in recognition of his battlefield bravery. Bird-in-Ground himself was modest about his exploits. He fought so hard, he explained, "because my address at the time I enlisted was in Oregon. I was afraid if I were killed in combat they would not bury me on the Crow Reservation in Montana. I was not trying to be a hero."

No matter. He was a hero to his people. Shortly after returning from the war, Bird-in-Ground was visited by the worried parents of a newborn son, Kenneth Old Coyote. Kenneth, they said, was critically ill and not expected to live. They appealed to Bird-in-Ground to visit their son in the Billings Hospital and pray for him. Having survived such a terrible battle, it was obvious God had blessed him, perhaps had given him special powers. Would he try to help their son? Andrew not only visited and prayed over the child but also gave him his new name "Kills Many Germans. Twenty years later, during the Vietnam War, Kills Many Germans Old Coyote earned the Bronze Star himself for saving two wounded comrades while under fire.

Like the Indian doughboys of the Great War, the Native Americans who fought in the Second World War had to cope with a great

Veterans form an honor guard at a ceremony on the Crow Reservation in May 1973. *Left to right:* Henry Old Coyote, Andrew Bird-in-Ground, Kenneth Old Coyote, and Joseph Medicine Crow. Courtesy Herman J. Viola.

deal of stereotyping in attitude and language from many of the non-Natives they encountered. Everything about them aroused curiosity, comment, and confusion, even their names. When Charles Kills the Enemy reported to his induction center and gave his name, he was told to get serious and give his real name. "But Kills the Enemy is my name," he tried to explain. Then there was the hospital nurse who, after checking the chart of a wounded soldier, exclaimed: "How on earth did you get shot with two arrows?" To which he replied, "That's my name, not my injury."

Invariably, white comrades often call Indian soldiers "Chief" or "Geronimo." The Indians usually took no offense since they realized the nicknames were not intended as racial insults but an acknowledgement of their reputed fighting abilities. What does offend Indian soldiers, however, is the continued use of the term "Indian Country" to designate anticipated areas of coming conflict with the United States' enemy. It certainly offended Sergeant Eli Painted Crow, a Yaqui soldier who served in Iraq. "At a military briefing we were warned of the dangers awaiting us in Indian Country," she noted in an interview on *Democracy Now!* "I'm standing there, just listening to this briefing, and I'm just in shock that after all this time, after so many Natives have served and are serving and are dying, we are still the enemy, even if we're wearing the same uniform."

Sources

Echohawk, Brummett, with Mark R. Ellenbarger. *Drawing Fire: A Pawnee, Artist, and Thunderbird in World War II.* Lawrence: University Press of Kansas, 2018.

Gladstone, Jack. "Remembering Private Charlo." In *Native Anthropology* (2010). YouTube, uploaded June 23, 2015. https://www.youtube.com/watch?v=dqsujA-L2ec.

Youngbull, Kristin M. *Brummett Echohawk: Pawnee Thunderbird and Artist.* Norman: University of Oklahoma Press, 2015.

CHAPTER 5

Counting Coup

Of the many cultural differences between Native and non-Native soldiers in World War II, few seemed more mysterious and impenetrable than the objects American Indian soldiers carried, such as feathers, medicine bundles, sweetgrass, and cedar. These and other sacred objects give the owners peace of mind as they face the perils of combat.

One soldier who revealed his use of sacred objects and prayers during combat, and who related his military experiences during World War II in his book *Counting Coup*, was Joseph Medicine Crow. Born on the Crow Reservation in 1913, Joseph was raised by pre–reservation era grandparents to be tough and strong like traditional Plains Indian warriors. "All the boys my age on the reservation were brought up in two ways at the same time," he wrote. "We were raised to be warriors but we were also expected to succeed in the white man's world."

The first Crow male to graduate from college—Bacone in Muskogee, Oklahoma—and the first to obtain a master's degree (in anthropology at the University of Southern California)—he was working on his doctorate before World War II interrupted his studies. Although offered a commission in the army because of his academic background, Joseph turned it down on the grounds that a warrior must first prove himself on the battlefield before leading others into battle. "It was the worst mistake I ever made," he laughs, "because the U.S. Army didn't work on the principles of the Crow Tribe and I never got another chance at a commission. I went into the Army a private and came out a private."

No matter. Private Medicine Crow distinguished himself on the battlefields of Germany. Joseph credits his success in combat to a special feather his uncle, Tom Yellowtail, gave to him. "It was a little, fluffy, snow-white eagle feather. Before a battle, I would put the feather inside my helmet. In addition to carrying the feather, I had to recite certain prayers and paint myself with a red lightning streak and red ring. I did not put the paint on my face but on my arms under my shirt. My uncle taught me how to paint myself properly. If I did not have paint, I could use a red pencil. That worked the same as paint."

When under fire, Joseph felt much more confident because of his special "medicine" and he credited that "medicine" for saving his life during several close encounters with the Germans. One such encounter occurred when his company came under artillery and mortar fire while marching on the side of a narrow valley. "The Germans were directly across from us," he recalls. "We were sitting ducks, but I felt pretty well prepared. My haversack was full of pemmican, a special treat of pounded meat that my mother had sent me. I had my rifle. I had painted the symbols on my arms, and I had put the medicine feather in my helmet. Suddenly, everything went black." An artillery shell had exploded right in front of him. The concussion of the blast knocked him out, and he fell off the cliff he was walking on.

When Joseph woke up, it was pitch dark. "I could hear guys moaning all around me," he remembers. "Miraculously, I was not hurt, just bruised a bit. But my helmet was gone. My medicine feather was gone. My haversack with the pemmican was gone. My rifle was gone. I felt helpless. I was in shock. It was so dark and the hill was so steep, I couldn't walk around. I had to crawl out of there. I began pulling myself up the hill by grabbing one tree and then another. First, I found my rifle. A little further up the hill I found my haversack. Near the last tree at the top of the hill, I found my helmet with the feather still tucked in the liner. When I put the helmet back on, I came to my senses. Everything was now all right, but I admit I had panicked there for a while. I have always attributed that particular sequence of good luck to my special Indian medicine. Whenever I had a close call, I would think about that medicine."

After Joseph returned from the war, he gave that feather to his cousin Henry Old Coyote, who was a machine gunner on a B-25 bomber. "That feather," Joseph says, "went with him to Africa, Germany, and Italy. I think after the Second World War that feather then went to Korea with a Crow soldier. It might have even gone to Vietnam. I don't know where it is now, but it certainly was powerful."

As Joseph relates in his memoir, while serving as an infantryman in Germany, he was able to perform the four types of war deeds, or "coups," a Crow warrior needed to earn in order to become a chief. The most significant, the most respected war deed was to sneak into an enemy camp at night, capture a prized horse, and then bring it back home. For such a bold exploit, the tribal elders would award the daring warrior a coup. The other coups were to touch a fallen enemy, to capture a weapon from an enemy, and to lead a successful war party. A successful war party was one in which the goals had been achieved and all the members returned safely. To become a Crow chief, a warrior had to perform at least one of each of the four war deeds, or coups.

When I went to Germany, I did not think in terms of counting coup. I believed those days were gone. Naturally, however, I thought about the famous Crow warriors of the past, of my grandfather Medicine Crow, who was one of the most famous of our war chiefs. I knew I had a legacy to live up to. My goal was to be a good soldier, to perform honorably in combat if the occasion should occur. But when I returned from Germany and the elders asked me and the other Crow warriors to tell our war stories, lo and behold, I had fulfilled the four requirements to be a chief.

I accomplished my first coup when the allies started the big push into Germany from France. It was January [1944] and the ground was covered with snow. The boundary that separated the two countries at this point was a little creek running through a canyon. It was a pretty deep canyon with steep walls. It was not rocky like our canyons in Montana, but it had real sharp hills.

That was the border. The French Maginot line, with its big guns, was behind us. On the other side of this creek, facing us, was the German Siegfried Line with its big guns.

Well, we went down the hill on the French side, crossed over into Germany and started toward the Siegfried Line. By now it was late afternoon. Before long we ran into foxholes just loaded with Germans. Then the fight started. After about an hour of fighting, it got dark, but we pushed forward. The Germans slowly withdrew up the side of their hill toward their big guns. As they retreated, we discovered a network of trenches higher than your head and about three or four feet wide, going every which way. We took the main trench and followed it to the top of the hill, but it was tough going. The path was kind of steep, slushy, and muddy.

By the time I got to the top, about 30 or 40 of our boys had gone ahead of me and they had made the ground even more sloppy and slippery. To make matters worse, the guy in front of me was a fat, clumsy kid. He was always slipping and falling. When we finally reached the crest of the hill, he couldn't make it over the top. He'd get there, almost to the top, then slide down. Finally, I managed to push him up and over. Just then, the Germans opened fire, and he came sliding back down again and landed on top of me. I think that is the only reason I didn't get killed myself that day. All the guys who had gotten on top were wiped out. The rest of us scattered. We went back down the hill into the side trenches and planned to stay there the rest of the night, but then the Germans began throwing hand grenades into the trenches.

The next day someone made the decision to blow up the concrete bunkers with the big guns where the Germans were hiding. As luck would have it, I was standing next to the Commanding Officer [CO] when the message came over the telephone. The message said to send some men back up the hill on the French side to get the boxes of dynamite needed to blow up the pill boxes. The CO said, "Well, chief"—he always called me chief—"I guess if anybody can get through, you can. Get six men and go up there."

Boy, it was a high hill, loaded with land mines, hidden bombs that would explode if you stepped on them.

Before I could ask for volunteers, my closest buddy stepped up and said, "Let's go, chief." In all, six guys, my closest friends, went with me. I was glad only six came forward because that made seven of us, and seven is one of the numbers considered lucky by Indians.

Before we left, the company commander ordered a smoke screen. "We can't afford to let these guys go in plain sight," he said, so guns from the American side began throwing smoke screen shells on the hill to give us cover. Pretty soon that whole hillside was covered with a mass of white smoke. Then we took off. We didn't know where the mines were. We just took off. Meanwhile, the Germans realized something was happening, so they began lobbing mortar shells on us, here and there. We made it, but it took a long time crawling up that hill. It was slippery with wet snow and steep, but at least we did not set off any of the land mines.

Anyhow, we finally got up there on the French side. The mess tent was still up and so was the communication center. We were given some hot soup and coffee, but not much time to rest, maybe half an hour, before they told us to take off again. They gave us boxes of dynamite with fuses. Each box weighed 50 pounds. We tried putting them on our shoulders, but the edges cut into our shoulders, and we couldn't walk down the hill carrying them in both hands. They were just too clumsy to handle. I didn't know what to do at first. Then I just sat down, set my box on my knees, and started sliding down the hill. The other guys saw me and did the same thing. Here we were, sliding behind one another down that hill. It wasn't fast, but we made it. Meanwhile, our boys had thrown some more smoke shells on the hillside to keep it foggy, but the Germans were lobbing mortar shells and hand grenades, too. If our boxes had gotten hit or if we had stepped on a mine, we would have been goners. It was a terrifying experience, but somehow we all came back without a scratch and with seven boxes of dynamite. The engineers then went ahead and blew up two or three of those big bunkers.

When I later told this story to the elders, they told me it was the same as leading a war party in the olden days. I had been assigned to a command job. We had returned safely and victoriously. We hadn't come back with horses or scalps, but we had returned with materials essential to the welfare of our men. That was my first war deed.

My next war deed was counting coup on a German soldier. After attacking the Siegfried Line, we were sent back to France for a couple of months of rest. Then, in March 1944, our unit went back into Germany. Soon after crossing the border we came to a little town. Our assignment was to enter the town from the rear, while other units attacked straight on. Boy, it was cold. There was still snow on the ground. To approach the town we had to wade through a slough up to our chests. I tell you it was wet and it was cold, but it was the safest way to get into town because the Germans had planted land mines all over. Because the Germans never expected anyone to come from that direction, we entered without them noticing us. In the meantime our boys who had gotten through the land mines had started hitting the other side of the town.

I had five or six soldiers assigned to me and we were told to secure a particular back alley. Although there was a lot of gunfire in the main street, the back alley where I was going was kind of quiet. With my platoon right behind me, I began running down the alley. I was carrying an M1 rifle. Along one side of the alley was a stone wall about 10 feet high. As I was running, I could see a gate, so I headed for it. I wanted to see what was happening on the main street. It turned out a German soldier had the same idea. He was running towards the gate, too, but from the other side of the wall. With all the shooting going on, I could not hear him and he could not hear me either. We met at the gate. My reactions were a bit quicker than his, and I was pretty spry in those days. I hit him under the chin with the butt of my rifle and knocked him down

Joseph Medicine Crow, who was awarded the Bronze Star and the French Legion of Honor for his military exploits, was named a war chief of the Crows because he performed the four required "coups" or war deeds against the Germans. These included capturing German horses. He is shown here about to enter the dance arena at the Crow Fair. He holds a horse dance stick, representing the horses he captured from German officers during World War II. Courtesy Herman J. Viola.

and sent his rifle flying. He landed on his back. He tried to reach for his rifle, but I kicked it out of the way. I dropped my rifle and jumped on top of him. As I sat on his chest, I grabbed his throat and started choking him. Meanwhile, the rest of my guys caught up. They wanted to shoot the German, but I still had my hands around his throat. He was scared. He began hollering, "Hitler Kaput! Hitler Kaput! Hitler nicht gut." He was crying. Tears were running down his face. I felt so sorry for him I gave him a cigarette and let him go.

Capturing that German counted for two war deeds. He was the first German we ran into that day, and by knocking him down and touching him I had counted coup on him. I had also taken his weapon away from him, which was another coup.

All that remained was capturing a horse, the most important coup. The war was almost over before I finally got my chance at a German horse. We were following a group of SS officers on horseback, about fifty of them. They had abandoned their men, who were surrendering by the thousands, hands up, throwing their rifles away. We followed these SS all night. They were riding their horses on an asphalt road and we could hear the clop, clop of the hooves ahead of us. About midnight, the horsemen left the highway and went to a farm about three miles down a dirt road. We followed their trail in the moonlight and arrived at a villa with a barn and a little fenced pasture.

As the CO sat down with the platoon leaders to discuss how best to handle the situation, all I could think about was those horses in the corral. The decision was made to attack the farmhouse at daybreak. As the CO started telling the platoon leaders to take their men this way and that way, I finally said: "Sir, maybe I should get those horses out of the corral before you attack because some of those SS guys might be able to escape on them. It would only take me about five minutes." The CO looked at me funny for a second, but he probably had an idea of what I was up to. "Okay, chief, you're on." That was all I needed. I took one of my buddies, and we began sneaking down towards the corral and the barn. We had to be careful in case a German was in the barn on guard duty, watching. When we got there, nothing was moving. The horses were tired, just standing around. I crawled through the corral fence and came up to one of them. I said, "Whoa. Whoa," in English. He snorted a little bit, but he quickly settled down. I had this rope with me that I used to tie my blanket. I took that rope and tied his lower jaw with a double half hitch, just like the old-time Crow warriors used to do, and then I tried to get on. But it was a tall horse, and my boots were so muddy and caked up, I had a hard time mounting. Finally, I led the horse to the watering trough and stood on that to get on its back.

I had told my buddy that I was going to the other end of the paddock behind the horses, and as soon as I got there I would give a little whistle. When he heard the whistle, he was to open the gate and get out of the way. Well, I got back there and whistled. Then I gave a Crow war cry and those horses took off. There were woods about a half mile away, so I headed that way. Just about that time, our boys opened fire on the farmhouse. By now it was coming daylight and I could get a good look at my horses. I had about 40 or 50 head. I was riding a sorrel with a blaze, a real nice horse. When we reached the woods and the horses started to mill around, I did something spontaneous. I sang a Crow praise song and rode around the horses. They all just looked at me.

The Germans had surrendered quickly and the firing was over, so I left the horses in the woods except the one I was riding and headed back to the farmhouse. After we had finished mopping things up and sending the prisoners to the rear, the company commander said, "Let's go," and we took off. There was a gravel railroad bed nearby, which made the walking a little better. As the guys took off down the railroad track, I was still on my horse. It was better to ride than walk. I felt good. I was a Crow warrior. My grandfathers would have been proud of me, I thought. But all too soon, the reality of the war came back. After letting me ride the horse for about a mile or so, the CO yelled over to me, "Chief, you better get off. You make too good a target."

The Crows also honor their veterans with celebrations and ceremonies. For example, whenever Crow soldiers returned to the reservation after World War II, their relatives would stage a welcome at the train station in the town of Lodge Grass and then host a grand reception about a week or two later. For Joseph Medicine Crow, his welcome-home reception in January 1946 was particularly memorable because he missed the gala awaiting him at the train station. En route his train stopped in Sheridan, Wyoming, for about a half hour

Joseph Medicine Crow at the grave of White Man Runs Him in the cemetery of the Little Bighorn National Monument. Courtesy Herman J. Viola.

so he took the opportunity to buy a hamburger at a favored diner. "Louie could make a dime hamburger taste like a New York–cut sirloin," Medicine Crow laughs. "Boy, I sure missed those hamburgers while I was overseas."

Because of the hamburgers he missed the train and the large crowd waiting to welcome him home. "My mother was ready with a stack of new Pendleton blankets to spread from the train to the singers, some sixty feet away. As I stepped off the train at Lodge Grass, I was supposed to walk along the row of blankets and start dancing as I reached the singers. Well, this didn't take place. Poor mom, she sure must have been disappointed."

As a result, Medicine Crow had to wait for his reception, which was held that weekend at the Tribal Dance Hall in Lodge Grass. "As I walked into the hall," he remembers vividly to this day,

people along the way shook my hand, relatives hugged me, and admiring girls kissed me. The drummers then sang the war honor song of my grandfather Chief Medicine Crow as I danced around the floor several times with my relatives following me. Then I had to tell everyone my combat experiences. It is a tradition known as 'The Recital of War Deeds.' At the time I did them, I did not think of them as 'coups,' except for capturing the horse. I knew that was special. Anyhow, several of the old-time chiefs were there listening, and when I finished telling my stories they talked among themselves and then declared that I had fulfilled all the requirements to become a Crow war chief, so then and there I became a chief.

After the reciting of the war deeds, my family started the giveaway, which is always done when someone in Crow society is honored. I know in white society when someone is honored that person gets the presents, but that is not the way Indians do it. When someone succeeds in our culture, he or she gives presents to those who helped make that success possible, like relatives, teachers, and friends. My mother gave away a stack of new Pendleton blankets, quilts, and other nice things. My dad gave away a fine horse with a new saddle and bridle in my honor. Then we had a big feast.

At that welcome-home reception, I also got a new name. One of my Whistling Water clansmen, Ties His Knees, and some others got together and decided to name me "High Bird," after one of our illustrious Whistling Water warriors. They also gave me his right to be a camp crier, or announcer, and they composed an honor song for me.

From that day to now, I use my honor song in all tribal ceremonies. When it is played I dance and my relatives follow me. The words in my honor song, like the songs of the Crow chiefs before me, reflect the pride we Crow people cherish to this day for our warrior heroes.

High Bird, you are a great soldier!
High Bird, you fought the mighty Metal Hats!
High Bird, you counted coup on them!
High Bird, you are a great soldier!

In the non-Native world, Joseph remained Joseph Medicine Crow, but to the Crow people, he was High Bird. I became aware of this when I had a meeting scheduled with him at a restaurant on the reservation. A Crow woman asked me, "Who are you looking for?" I said Joseph Medicine Crow. "Oh," she replied, "you mean High Bird." Years later, when he adopted me as his brother, he gave me the

After Joseph Medicine Crow received the Presidential Medal of Freedom at a White House ceremony on August 12, 2009, the group moved to a private room where he played a hand drum and sang an honor song to Barack and Michelle Obama in appreciation. Standing at left is Leonard Bends, a spiritual leader of the Crow people. Photo courtesy The White House.

name of his grandfather One Star and whenever we exchanged letters it was always between High Bird and One Star.

Sources

Echohawk, Brummett, with Mark R. Ellenbarger. *Drawing Fire: A Pawnee Artist and Thunderbird in World War II.* Lawrence: University of Kansas Press, 2018.

Kaplan, Sarah. "Joe Medicine Crow, a War Chief, Historian, and Last Link to the Battle of the Little Big Horn, Dies at 102." *Washington Post,* April 4, 2016.

Medicine Crow, Joseph. *Counting Coup: Becoming a Crow Chief on the Reservation and Beyond.* Washington, DC: National Geographic Society, 2006.

Viola, Herman J. *Warriors in Uniform: The Legacy of American Indian Heroism.* Washington, DC: National Geographic Society, 2008.

Youngbull, Kristin M. *Brummett Echohawk: Pawnee Thunderbird and Artist.* Norman: University of Oklahoma Press, 2015.

CHAPTER 6

Code Talking

The Warriors' Secret Weapon

Even before the attack on Pearl Harbor thrust the United States into another world war, the US Army initiated a formal training program based on the Code Talkers' success in World War I and began recruiting Native speakers from various tribes, including the Chippewa (Ojibwe), Comanche, Meskwaki, and Oneida, to transmit messages on the battlefield. An interesting and largely unknown side note is that Hitler in the 1930s, facing the possibility of an another world war, sent German "scholars" into Indian Country to study Native languages in an attempt to foil their use should the United States enter the pending conflict. The effort failed because the American Indian languages the Germans found were not written but only oral.

The most celebrated and publicized Code Talkers of World War II were the Navajos. As John Goodluck Sr., one of the Code Talkers, later recalled, a test was conducted on the reservation for navy officials who were somewhat skeptical about using Indians to send secret communications. For the test, he said, the military placed radios 300 to 400 yards apart and sent coded messages using both Navajo Code Talkers and regular Morse code machines. "The Code Talkers deciphered the messages in under a minute. The machines took an hour," Goodluck laughed.

Code Talker messages were strings of seemingly unrelated Navajo words. The Code Talkers would translate each word into English, and then decipher the message by using only the first letter of each English word. For example, several Navajo words could be used to represent the letter *a*—"wol-la-chee" (ant), "be-la-sana" (apple), or "tse-nill" (ax). While the Navajos used more than one word to

A two-man team of Navajo Code Talkers relay orders over a
field radio in the Pacific theater. Courtesy National Museum
of the American Indian, Smithsonian Institution.

represent letters, about 450 common military terms had no equiv-
alent and so had assigned code words. For example, "division"
was "ashih-hi" (salt); "America" was "Ne-he-mah" (Our mother);
"fighter plane" was "da-he-tih-hi" (hummingbird); "submarine"
became "besh-lo" (iron fish); and "tank destroyer" was "chay-da-
gahi-nail-tsaidi" (tortoise killer).

After the Navajo code was developed, the Marine Corps established a code-talking school. As the war progressed, more than four
hundred Navajos were eventually recruited as Code Talkers. The
training was intense. Following their basic training, the Code Talkers
completed extensive training in communication and memorization
of the code.

However, the Navajos, Comanches, Hopis, and Meskwakis also
developed and used special codes based on their distinct languages.

According to historian William Meadows, these became known as Type One codes. As Meadows explains in *Comanche Code Talkers of World War II*, "The use of Native American languages with specifically designed encoded terms can be classified as Type One, ... while the use of Native American languages without specifically designed encoded terms can be classified as Type Two codes." The Type Two codes are explained later.

To develop their Type One code, the original twenty-nine Navajo Code Talkers created a dictionary that provided a Navajo word for each letter of the English alphabet. Since they had to memorize all the words, they used things that were familiar to them such as animals, birds, and various features of the natural world.

Letter	Navajo word	English word
C	MOASI	cat
D	LHA-CHA-EH	dog
E	DZEH	elk
I	TKIN	ice
O	NE-AHS-JAH	owl
R	GAH	rabbit
V	A-KEH-DI-GLINI	victor

Here is a coded message:

MOASI NE-AHS-JAH LHA-CHA-EH DZEH GAH DZEH MOASI DZEH TKIN A-KEH-DI-GLINI DZEH LHA-CHA-EH

This is the English translation:

C-O-D-E R-E-C-E-I-V-E-D

Because the Native soldiers had to develop special words for World War II military equipment, such as types of planes, ships, or weapons, they received picture charts that showed the items. After looking at the pictures, they came up with words that seemed to fit the pictures.

Code Talkers did more than speak into hand-held radios or phones. They had to know how to operate both wire and radio equipment, which they often had to carry on their backs. They also needed to know how to set up and maintain the electronic communication wires or lines. Sometimes their messages were broadcast over a wide area, helping to direct big operations such as large-scale troop movements; at other times, their communication related to a small operation such as a patrol.

Code Talkers received their messages in English, which they translated and then sent to another Code Talker. After being transmitted and received, the message was written down in English and entered into a message logbook. The Code Talkers also sent messages in English.

All told, 379 Navajo talkers served in the Pacific theater, while Code Talkers from other tribes served in the European theater. Charles Chibitty, the last survivor of the Comanche Code Talkers, who died in July 2005, said two Comanches were assigned to each of the 4th Infantry Division's three regiments. They sent coded messages from the front line to division headquarters, where other Comanches decoded the messages. Chibitty, who joined the army in January 1941 along with twenty other Comanches, said they compiled a vocabulary of about 250 military terms during basic training at Fort Benning, Georgia. "Machine gun" became "sewing machine," Chibitty recalled, "because of the noise the sewing machine made when my mother was sewing." Since there was no Comanche word for "tank," the Code Talkers used their word for "turtle." "Bomber" became "pregnant airplane." "Hitler" was "Posah-tai-vo," or "Crazy White Man." Chibitty recalled that the first message he sent on D-Day using the code the Comanches had created was, after translation into English: "Five miles to the right of the designated area and five miles inland the fighting is fierce and we need help."

Type Two codes were messages sent in everyday tribal language. For example, a message such as, "We need more ammunition," would just be spoken in a Native language over the radio. Typical of Type Two Code Talkers were the Crow brothers Henry Old Coyote and Barney Old Coyote Jr. Although brothers were not supposed to serve together, their mother requested an exception be made for her sons. The Army Air Corps complied, and Henry, who was nine years older, promised their mother that he would look after Barney, who had just graduated from high school.

Both brothers joined the Army Air Corps and flew combat missions aboard B-17 Flying Fortresses over France, North Africa, Italy, Norway, and Berlin. Although bomber crews were under strict orders to maintain radio silence, Barney could radio messages in the Crow language back to his brother Henry's plane and share information about targets and enemy strength in order to baffle German code breakers. As Barney explained, "I would give a fake target in English to Henry in a following plane and then give him the actual target in our Crow language. That confused the Germans and reduced our casualties by quite a bit, which made for successful bombing runs time after time. We weren't Code Talkers. We spoke Crow. We did what we knew. We were Wind Talkers."

As a tail gunner, waist gunner and engineer riding in the top turret, Barney had the main assignment of shooting at German planes and attacking troops on the ground. "It was always terrifying," he confessed. "On raids, 500 planes might fly out, but only 200 would return. Surviving planes came back riddled with bullet holes. After a while, we stopped counting all the holes."

Barney flew seventy-two combat missions and gained a reputation for being a good marksman. So good, in fact, that for his success in shooting down German planes and for bravery in combat, he became the most decorated American Indian in World War II, earning seventeen awards: the Distinguished Flying Cross, the Air Medal with fourteen oak-leaf clusters, and the Silver Star.

CODE TALKER RECOGNITION

Despite their sacrifices and important roles in winning the war, Code Talkers for many years failed to receive recognition for their service. A key reason was the program's secrecy. The US government did not declassify the program until 1968. As Chester Nez, one of the original twenty-nine Navajo Code Talkers revealed in an interview at the National Museum of the America Indian in 2004, "When we got out, discharged, they told us this thing that you guys did is going to be a secret. When you get home you don't talk about what you did; don't tell your people, your parents, family. Never, never, don't mention, don't talk about it. And that was our secret for about twenty-five, twenty-six years until August 16, 1968. That's when it was declassified. Then it was open. I told my sister, my aunt, all my families what I really did."

Only then did people begin to realize the importance of the Code Talkers' achievements, and only then did they begin to receive the recognition they merited. In 1989, the French government awarded the Comanche Code Talkers the Chevalier of the National Order of Merit, its highest honor. Not until 2000 did the United States Congress pass legislation to honor the Navajo Code Talkers. The act provided gold medals to the original twenty-nine Navajos who developed the code, and silver medals to those who served later in the program. A statement in the Navajo language on the obverse of the medals translates to: "With the Navajo language they defeated the enemy."

Although the Navajo Code Talkers were awarded congressional medals in 2001, the Code Talkers from the other thirty-three tribes had to wait another seven years before their vital contributions to the war effort were formally recognized with passage of Public Law 110-420. The act authorized the US Mint to strike a unique Congressional Gold Medal for each tribe that had a member who served as a Code Talker in either World War I or II. Silver duplicate medals were to be presented

The Navajo Code Talkers Medal. Centered along the bottom
is the inscription "Diné Bizaad Yee Atah Naayéé' Yik'eh
Deesdl íí," which means "The Navajo Language Was
Used to Defeat the Enemy." Courtesy US Mint.

to the specific Code Talkers, their next of kin, or other personal representatives. In addition, bronze duplicates were made available for sale to the public.

The actual awarding of the medals took place in a dramatic ceremony in Emancipation Hall in the US Capitol Visitor Center on November 20, 2013, when twenty-five tribes received their gold medals. The remaining eight other tribes, although honored at the ceremony, had to wait until their medals were designed and struck, a process that continues to this day. Following the ceremony at a reception held at the National Museum of the American Indian, director Kevin Gover, whose grandfather Phillip was one of the Pawnee Code Talkers in World War II, noted that despite nearly two centuries of effort, the Bureau of Indian Affairs had not yet managed to eradicate Indian languages. Gover marveled "that [with]in just two or three generations of being in conflict with the United States, our warriors would go forward and play such a crucial role in the victory over this country's enemies."

ANDREW PERRY

Buried along with 860 other soldiers in the Rhone American Military Cemetery in Draguignan, France, is Andrew Perry, one of four Choctaw Code Talkers who served in World War II. The other three, all of whom survived the war, were Schlicht Billy, Davis Pickens, and Forreston Baker.

Most of the servicemen buried in the cemetery were members of the US Seventh Army, in particular the 45th Infantry Division (the Thunderbirds), who died in the late summer of 1944 during Operation Dragoon, the allied invasion of southern France, often cited as the Second D-Day. Launched on August 15, 1944, from the Mediterranean Sea, the operation's primary goal was to open a second battle front in France, forcing the Axis powers to divert forces from the Normandy combat zone in northern France that facilitated the Allied push into Western Europe. The strategy worked.

Perry, who was nineteen when he enlisted in the army, had not learned English until he went to school. In a letter to his sister while in basic training, he wrote: "We will pull out of here someday, to where I

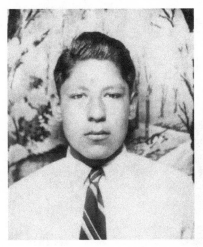

Andrew Perry, as a civilian and as a private in the
US Army. Courtesy Debbie Cheshewalla.

don't know and don't care. We should of already been in Ireland but it was changed and so we are still here, waiting anxiously to move away from here which I hope we do before it gets too cold here." One of the things he enjoyed doing was marching. "Did you listen to the Chicago Bears and Eastern All-stars play football? It was played at Boston. Well we paraded there before it started, two platoons of full blooded Indians from Oklahoma, and watched the game. I have paraded before many important people and large crowds especially at New York where I enjoyed it the most."

Perry wrote his last letter home March 11, 1944, five months before his death. "Dear Sis, Still battling here in Italy and mighty tired of it but can't give up. I've lived through several months of fighting but still that's no sign I'll be able to go home as anything can happen any moment, but I never do let that worry me as if it's my time I'll go. Andrew."

The people of Draguignan, like most French citizens, remain deeply grateful for the ultimate sacrifice that so many American military personnel made in the liberation of France during World War II. An

Students of the Jean Moulin Lycée with their gift to Debbie Cheshewalla, who is standing at right, holding the bouquet of flowers. Next to her is her cousin Chad Renfro. Courtesy Herman J. Viola.

example of this gratitude is the Souvenir Franco-Americain (SFA), or Franco-American Society, which was founded in Draguignan on August 16, 1968. Every Memorial Day since its founding, the society has honored the memory of a service member buried in the Rhone American Military Cemetery by inviting and hosting two family members of the fallen American. For Memorial Day 2018 the Franco-American Society invited Andrew Perry's niece Debbie Cheshewalla, who lives in Oklahoma, and her cousin Chad Renfro, an Osage.

When the students at Jean Moulin Lycée, the junior high school across the street from the Rhone Cemetery, learned that Debbie was coming to visit her uncle's grave, they created a gift for her—a large poster featuring pictures of Andrew, a Choctaw Code Talker commemorative medal, a Totem Pole, an American tank, and the Rhone Cemetery with the US flag flying above the chapel.

CODE TALKER THOMAS BEGAY

Michelle Pearson

Military service for Thomas H. Begay started early in his life in northern Arizona when he was simply looking for work but was turned down for a job due to his age. Begay got angry. "That guy made me mad," he says. "I told that person I'm going to join the Marines and show them I'm old enough to fight the Japanese. If I'm old enough to fight, then I could be working." That simple moment led Begay to the enlistment office and resulted in a legacy of service in the United States Marines and, later, in the United States Army—and a lifetime of honor, commitment to his country, the Navajo Nation, and most importantly his family.

Begay was born on February 5, 1926, in the US Southwest, an area where tribal lands are common. He grew up speaking Navajo in a remote community near Two Wells, Chi Chil-Tah, and the Jones Ranch, close to Gallup, New Mexico. He learned English when he was sent to school at Fort Defiance, Arizona.

At age sixteen he enlisted in the US Marine Corps. He served in the 5th Marine Division Signal Company and in the Radio Section of the H & S Company, 27th Marines, famous for its work transmitting more than eight hundred messages during the capture of Iwo Jima. Those messages, transmitted around the clock on six different Navajo-language networks, were important factors in the capturing and then holding of Iwo Jima by American forces for over five weeks. He was honorably discharged in 1946 as a lance corporal.

During the Korean War, Begay once again joined the military, this time with the 7th Infantry Division of the US Army. He served as a parachutist and glider man during combat and survived the Choisin Reservoir Battle in North Korea. After his honorable discharge in 1953, he moved to New Mexico and Arizona to raise a family of three sons and a daughter with his wife, Nonabah Doris Yazzie Begay. All of his children have followed their father's footsteps and served in the US armed forces.

Begay's service to his country did not stop with his service to the military. He served more than forty years with the Bureau of Indian Affairs (US Department of the Interior), coordinating programs that served the Navajo Nation. He also served his tribal community as an active member of the local school board, and he started the Navajo Youth Baseball League in Chinle, Arizona, along with many other programs and efforts to preserve, honor, and protect the culture and language of the Navajo Nation.

Begay is the recipient of many honors, including the Presidential Unit Citation with three Bronze Stars and the Meritorious Unit Citation with the Korean Service Medal, bearing five Bronze Stars. In 2001, he received the Congressional Medal of Honor from President George W. Bush in a ceremony in Washington, DC.

Sources

Bureau of Indian Affairs. "Thomas H. Begay." Washington, DC: US Department of the Interior, 2018.

Jevic, Adam. "Semper Fidelis, Code Talkers." *Prologue Magazine* (National Archives), Winter 2001.

Gladstone, Jack. "Navajo Code Talkers." In *Noble Heart*. BSG Productions, 1995. YouTube, uploaded September 4, 2006. https://www .youtube.com/watch?v=YZuOiqo1glk.

Holiday, Samuel, and Robert M. McPherson *Under the Eagle: Samuel Holiday, Navajo Code Talker*. Norman: University of Oklahoma Press, 2013.

Meadows, William C. *Comanche Code Talkers of World War II*. Austin: University of Texas Press, 2002.

Meadows, William C. *The First Code Talkers: Native American Communicators in World War I*. Norman: University of Oklahoma Press, 2021.

Nez, Chester, with Judith Schiess Avila. *Code Talker*. New York: Penguin, 2011.

Schontzler, Gail. "Barney Old Coyote: Warrior, Educator, Indian Rights Advocate." *Bozeman Daily Chronicle*, August 12, 2014.

Silversmith, Shondiin. "Navajo Code Talker Thomas H. Begay Wanted to Be a Gunner: Here's How He Became a Code Talker." *Arizona Republic*, August 29, 2019.

Viola, Herman J. *Warriors in Uniform*. Washington, DC: National Geographic Society, 2008.

Viola, Herman J., and Susan P. Viola. "Are There Any American Indians Buried Here?" *Tidewater Times*, February 2019.

CHAPTER 7

The Cold War

Immediately following World War II, another war began. Known as the Cold War, it dominated the second half of the twentieth century, from the Berlin Airlift in 1947 to the tearing down of the Berlin Wall forty years later. The Cold War had its hot moments, notably in Korea and Vietnam, where the United States sought to prevent the anticipated expansion of communism into Southeast Asia. Both North Korea and North Vietnam were connected to communist China, which provided its neighbors with supplies, ammunition, and other support. South Korea and South Vietnam on the other hand, favored democracy. According to the "domino theory" that justified United States participation in those conflicts, if South Korea and then South Vietnam fell under communist control, neighboring nations would also be at risk.

America's Native peoples paid scant heed to the geopolitical implications of the Cold War. Their country needed fighting men, and they answered the call. No matter their adversaries, Native Americans again enlisted in numbers that far exceeded their percentage of the American population. Although exact figures are difficult to establish, it is believed 10,000 Indians served and 194 died in Korea. In Vietnam, 42,000 served and 226 died.

Both wars were bloody and brutal. After three years of inconclusive fighting that caused the combat deaths of almost 37,000 Americans, the Korean War ended in a truce at the point where it had started. In Vietnam, a war that lasted ten years, 58,000 American soldiers died. The Korean War witnessed short bursts of intense fighting, whereas the fighting in Vietnam tended to be long and drawn out, creating fervent anti-war sentiment in the United States. As a result, there was an enormous difference between how the veterans of each war were received at home when the fighting ended.

Overshadowed by World War II and Vietnam, the Korean War is often referred to as the "Forgotten War." It began June 25, 1950, when North Korean troops crossed the 38th parallel dividing the Korean Peninsula, and it featured some of the most vicious fighting and worst conditions American soldiers ever experienced in combat. Although China, the United States, and the United Nations agreed to an armistice in 1953, South Korea refused to sign, leaving the two Koreas separate and the war in suspension to this day.

One of the American Indians who served in the Korean conflict was Ben Nighthorse Campbell, a Northern Cheyenne who later became one of the few Native Americans ever to serve in the US Congress. A high school dropout, Campbell joined the air force in 1951 and spent a year in a police unit in Korea. Like other warriors in uniform, he greatly valued his military experience. "There was a camaraderie that transcends ethnicity when you serve your country overseas in wartime," says Campbell, who served two terms as a member of the US House of Representatives, then two terms as a US senator from Colorado, and whose legislative efforts helped establish the National Museum of the American Indian. "Yes," Campbell says, "I am American and I am Indian and I am a vet. I believe I was compelled to serve to honor the warrior tradition which is inherent to most Native American societies—the pillars of strength, honor, pride, devotion, and wisdom."

BEN NIGHTHORSE CAMPBELL

Michelle Pearson

Ask Ben Nighthorse Campbell about the jobs he has held in his varied career and his answer will probably be rancher, jeweler, senator, soldier, father, and grandfather, among others. His service record is impressive and varied in the United States, and his legacy, as a member

Senator Ben Nighthorse Campbell became a star judo athlete after his service in the Korean War. Each of the eagle feathers in his warbonnet represents one of his judo victories. Courtesy Herman J. Viola.

of the Northern Cheyenne Nation, a soldier who served in the Korean War, and as a US senator from Colorado, is only part of his story.

Born in Auburn, California, in 1933 to a Portuguese mother and a Northern Cheyenne father, he dropped out of high school to enlist in the United States Air Force and serve as an air policeman during the Korean War. He was recognized with several awards for his service, including the Korean Service Medal and the Air Medal. While in the air force, Campbell completed his GED. After leaving the air force, he earned a degree in physical education and the arts. At this time, in a traditional naming ceremony held by his tribe, he adopted the middle name Nighthorse to honor his Northern Cheyenne heritage.

Campbell competed in judo after training extensively in Japan and participated in the 1964 Olympics. Because of an injury, he did not win a medal, but the impact of his training and life in Japan during the games led to his work after the Olympics as the US men's national judo coach while teaching physical education and art. Meanwhile, he continued to design jewelry by combining the Northern Cheyenne traditions with Japanese artistic influences.

After Campbell met Linda Price, they were married and moved to Ignacio, Colorado, in 1978. Shortly thereafter he became involved in politics and, in 1982, was elected to the US House of Representatives for the first time. After serving two terms, he was elected to the US Senate. A longtime Democrat, he switched to the Republican Party in 1995, which surprised many voters. But he won reelection as US senator from Colorado in 1998 by wide margin. He retired in 2005 and continued to work in governmental policy as a lobbyist.

Ben Nighthorse Campbell was instrumental in establishing the Sand Creek Massacre National Historic Site with passage of Public Law 105-243, which he sponsored. The site was dedicated in 2007. At that dedication, when a middle school student from the Preserve America Youth Summit asked him how he felt about the dedication, he stated, "It is our actions that move forward the process of healing of a nation. It is also our actions that ensure that the conflicts of the past are remembered and do not get repeated. It is our duty to remember the voices that are often unheard so that we have a better future as a country."

Five Native North Americans and two Native Hawaiians received the Congressional Medal of Honor for heroism in Korea. One was Private First Class Charles George, a Cherokee from North Carolina, who sacrificed his life by throwing himself on a hand grenade to protect his fellow soldiers. Another was Captain Raymond Harvey, a Chickasaw, who led his platoon against entrenched positions, personally killing several of the enemy with carbine fire and hand grenades and then, though wounded, refusing to be evacuated until his company's objective had been achieved. The third recipient was Sergeant Tony Burris, a Choctaw, who charged an enemy machine gun emplacement, sacrificing his life to save his comrades. The fourth to receive the medal was Corporal Mitchell Red Cloud Jr., a Ho-Chunk from Wisconsin and a veteran of World War II. Corporal Red Cloud, a member of Company E, 24th Infantry, sacrificed his life while enabling his company to evacuate wounded comrades. He received the Medal of Honor posthumously on July 2, 1951. The granite stela of the monument erected in his honor at Black River Falls, Wisconsin, is inscribed with the statement, "The son of a Winnebago chief and warriors who believe that when a man goes into battle, he expects to kill or be killed and if he dies he will live forever."

The fifth recipient was Woodrow Wilson Keeble, who performed remarkable exploits on the battlefields of both World War II and the Korean War. A member of the Wahpeton Sisseton Sioux Tribe of North Dakota, Sergeant Keeble earned five Purple Hearts, two Bronze Stars, a Silver Star, and a Distinguished Service Cross. Although his men twice recommended him for the Congressional Medal of Honor, no action was taken during his lifetime, but he did receive it posthumously, on March 3, 2008.

Orphaned at age nine, Keeble spent most of his youth at the Wahpeton Indian Boarding School in North Dakota and then returned there after his military service. An exceptional athlete, he was being recruited by the Chicago White Sox as a pitcher when called to service in World War II. He saw combat throughout the South Pacific with the North Dakota Army National Guard's 164th Infantry Regiment, and he earned a well-deserved reputation for taking care of his men. As one recalled, "The safest place to be was next to Woody." In fact, he garnered his first Purple Heart and first Bronze Star on Guadalcanal while attempting to rescue several fellow soldiers.

When the Korean War broke out, Keeble reenlisted. Asked why, he said, "Somebody has to teach these kids how to fight." Keeble returned to service at age thirty-four as a master sergeant. And it was from the Korean War that he emerged as the most decorated military hero in North Dakota history. To his comrades in arms he seemed fearless: "As often seen in movies but seldom seen on the actual place of combat," wrote Sergeant Joe Sagami.

Keeble's defining moment came on October 20, 1951, during Operation Nomad, the last major US offensive of the war, as his company battled Communist Chinese troops near Kumsong. Two days earlier he had engaged the enemy in a firefight for which he would later receive the Silver Star. Now, though already wounded twice and suffering from a badly injured knee, Keeble ignored requests from medics and his men to remain behind when his company was ordered to take a nearby hill. Not until they had nearly reached the top, however, did the soldiers realize that they had climbed into an inescapable trap with entrenched enemy troops directly above them. "They were throwing so many grenades at us," one of the trapped soldiers remembers, "it looked like a flock of blackbirds flying over."

Keeble took matters into his own hands. Armed only with an M-1 rifle and hand grenades, he crawled toward the enemy and waged a one-man battle. Thanks to his pitching skill, he managed to destroy three machine gun bunkers with well-aimed hand grenades, killing nine Chinese and wounding the other crew members. Although hit multiple times during this assault, including a concussion grenade that stunned him a moment, he then attacked two trenches filled with enemy troops, killing seven before the rest ran away. On the back side of the entrenchments, his soldiers found a Chinese command post, which explained why the enemy had fought so fiercely. For this exploit, Keeble received the Distinguished Service Cross.

Although he had fragmentation wounds in his chest, both arms, and his left thigh, right calf, right knee, and right thigh, Keeble refused to evacuate, because no replacements were available. He returned to duty even though his wounds were bleeding through his bandages, he was badly limping, and he was so weak, he could hardly lift his rifle. Little wonder that there was such a determined effort to get Sergeant Keeble the medal he so richly deserved.

Following his service in Korea, Keeble returned to the Wahpeton Indian School, where he held several positions until a series of strokes rendered him speechless and unable to work. Hard times forced him to pawn some of his medals. He died in 1982 at the age of sixty-five and is buried in Sisseton, South Dakota. "It's hard to believe he had the warrior-like capabilities, because outside of a war setting, he was so likeable," said Kurt Blue Dog, one of his relatives.

The two Native Hawaiians who earned the medal, both posthumously, were Privates Anthony T. Kaho'ohanohano and Herbert Kailieha Pililaau. Private Kaho'ohanohano was in charge of a machine gun squad tasked with supporting another company near Chup'a-ri, Korea, when a numerically superior enemy force launched an attack, forcing him and his squad to withdraw to a more defensible position. Although wounded in the shoulder, he ordered his men to hold their ground while he gathered ammunition and returned to their original post, where he single-handedly held off the enemy advance. After running out of ammunition, he grabbed an entrenching tool and fought hand to hand with the enemy soldiers until they killed him. When American soldiers retook the position, they found thirteen dead Chinese soldiers lying around Private Kaho'ohanohano's body. His family received the Medal of Honor at a White House ceremony on May 2, 2011.

During the Battle of Heartbreak Ridge, Herbert Kailieha Pililaau voluntarily stayed behind to cover his unit's withdrawal in the face of an intense North Korean attack. Using his automatic rifle and hand grenades, he held off the attackers until he ran out of ammunition. Then, like Private Kaho'ohanohano, he engaged the attackers in hand-to-hand combat until being overrun and killed by bayonet. When his comrades retook the position the next day, they found forty dead enemy soldiers around his body. For his heroism, Private Pililaau was posthumously awarded the Medal of Honor on June 18, 1952. He is the first Native Hawaiian to have received that award.

Three American Indians earned the Congressional Medal of Honor in Vietnam. Each certainly displayed "conspicuous gallantry and intrepidity at the risk of life above and beyond the call of duty."

One was master sergeant and Green Beret Raul P. "Roy" Benavidez, a Yaqui Indian from Texas. Although badly wounded in 1965,
during his first tour of duty in Vietnam, he recovered after intense
rehabilitation and requested a return to Vietnam where, on May 2,
1968, he volunteered to help rescue by helicopter a dozen wounded
soldiers who were surrounded by a large force of North Vietnamese.
Armed with only a knife, he jumped from the helicopter and ran
through gunfire, suffering wounds to his leg, face, and head to help
carry wounded soldiers to the hovering copter. During the rescue
the helicopter pilot was shot and the aircraft crashed. Benavidez then
pulled the wounded out of the overturned aircraft and directed air
strikes on the surrounding enemy while waiting for a second helicopter to arrive. When it landed, Benavidez helped load the wounded
on board while under intense gunfire. At one point, a North Vietnamese soldier clubbed him from behind. Benavidez killed him and
then managed to retrieve classified documents from the body of the
team's leader before being pulled up into the helicopter and flying
off to safety. Covered in blood and presumed dead, Benavidez was
being placed inside a body bag at the base camp when he spit in a
doctor's face to prove he was still alive. At his Medal of Honor ceremony at the White House in 1981 President Ronald Reagan said,
"If the story of Master Sergeant Benavidez's heroism were a movie
script, you would not believe it."

Another medal winner was Boatswain's Mate First Class James E.
Williams, a Cherokee who enlisted in the navy at the age of sixteen
upon graduation from high school and saw service in both Korea and
Vietnam. In Vietnam, Petty Officer First Class Williams commanded
River Patrol Boat 105, tasked with intercepting supplies intended for
the North Vietnamese Army and protecting people living along the
Mekong River Delta. On October 31, 1966, while searching for Vietcong in a remote area of the delta, Williams discovered a large enemy
base, resulting in a fierce firefight that lasted several hours and did
not end until helicopter assistance arrived. All told, the American
forces destroyed more than sixty-five enemy boats. For his actions

Master Sergeant Raul "Roy" Perez Benavidez, US Army Special Forces, wearing the Medal of Honor he received for his valorous actions in combat near Loc Ninh, South Vietnam, on May 2, 1968. Courtesy Roy P. Benavidez Estate.

that day, Williams was awarded the Medal of Honor. When he retired the following year, his awards included not only the Medal of Honor but also the Navy Cross, two Silver Stars, three Bronze Stars, and three Purple Hearts, plus numerous commendation and combat action medals and ribbons, making him the most decorated enlisted man in the history of the US Navy. To complete the honors accorded Williams, who died in 1999, the navy named an Arleigh Burke–class destroyer commissioned in 2004 the USS *James E. Williams*.

Petty Officer Second Class Michael E. Thornton, a navy SEAL of Cherokee descent, earned his Medal of Honor in the waning days of the Vietnam War. On the evening of October 31, 1972, Thornton was with four other men, one of whom was his commanding officer, Lieutenant Thomas R. Norris. The team had gone on a mission in a junk to capture prisoners and gather intelligence but landed by mistake in North Vietnam. As they tried to return to the coast in the morning, they were spotted by a group of enemy soldiers, beginning a five-hour battle in which Lieutenant Norris was severely wounded. Thornton ran through heavy fire to rescue Norris. He then carried the unconscious SEAL into the water and began swimming out to sea. When one of the other men in their group, now in the water with him, was also wounded, Thornton supported him as well, swimming with the two injured men for more than two hours before being rescued by the same junk that had dropped them off the night before. What made the exploit even more unique is that Lieutenant Norris had himself earned the Medal of Honor for heroism in Vietnam a few months earlier.

Of the 42,000 Indians who served in the military during the Vietnam era, 135 were members of the Crow Nation of Montana, including Carson Walks Over Ice, a nephew of Joseph Medicine Crow. Carson, who died in 2011, had grown up listening to stories about the great Crow warriors of the past. He volunteered to go to Vietnam because he wanted to live up to the warrior traditions of his people.

As Carson explained, "I felt I had an advantage over the non-Native soldiers in Vietnam because of my Indian heritage. The spirit world is very important to us, and it is hard to find anyone among us who does not believe in the 'One Above,' the creator." Three Native spiritual powers protected Carson and gave him peace of mind. One was a medal with wings on it that he received from his grandmother and wore around his neck. Another one, made for him by a Crow medicine woman, he wore on a string around his waist. During one firefight, Carson lost both of them. A bullet ripped away the medal hanging around his neck; another bullet took off the one tied around his waist. "But those medicines protected me," Carson said. "Neither bullet hurt me and, hard as it is to believe, the medicine that had been tied around my waist came home, all the way back to Pryor, Montana, without me. The woman who made it said that it just appeared one day. These things happen. Non-Indians can't understand them, but they happen."

The third spiritual power that gave him comfort was a Sun Dance ceremony in which one of his uncles prayed for his safe return.

Carson Walks Over Ice was a Green Beret during the Vietnam War. His safe return was predicted in the Sun Dance, a sacred ceremony of the Crow people. Courtesy Herman J. Viola.

"Because I was going overseas, my uncle danced for me, and after the ceremony I went to him to give him cigarettes and all the other things that you give to a sun dancer. As I walked up, he said, 'I saw you on crutches standing in the sunlight at the entrance to Sun Dance lodge.'" Carson knew then that he was going to be hurt, but that he would return from Vietnam. "And, in fact, the next time my uncle saw me," Carson said, "I was on crutches because I had been shot through the leg. Those three things, the two medicines and the Sun Dance, they protected me. They brought me back."

For Indian soldiers the warrior tradition provides a common bond, a shared brotherhood in the US military even with members of tribes that once were traditional enemies. For example, Carson and Richard Spider, of the Sioux Nation—once mortal enemies of the Crow—became brothers in Vietnam. "For some reason," Carson said, "it was army policy not to put Indians together. For example, there were four Indians in my company, one in each of the four platoons. I was in the first platoon, my brother Richard was in the second, a Ponca in the third, and a Klamath in the fourth. Even though we were often separated, it was great having Native soldiers nearby. Whenever we saw see each other, we would say, 'Hey.' That's a difference between Indian and non-Indian soldiers. When Indians see each other, it's like old home week. It made no difference if we were not next to each other in the field because Indians talk with their hands, in sign language. We understand each other in sign. The non-Indian soldiers would see us doing it and say, 'What are you doing?' I'd say, 'I'm talking to him.' Even though we were 100 yards apart we could talk to each other."

For Carson, the worst thing that happened in Vietnam was fellow soldier Richard Spider's death. "We did everything together. We were in the same company and fought in the same battles. Our last battle was May 18, 1967." While on a search-and-destroy mission their company was ambushed. "The enemy wiped us out. Three of the four Indians in our company went down. Richard and the Klamath were killed, and my right leg was shattered. The Ponca was the only Indian left standing that day. Richard was due to be discharged in three weeks."

Soon after Carson got home, following hospital stays in the Philippines, Okinawa, Japan, and finally Denver, he visited Richard's family at Fort Thompson in South Dakota. There the Spider family adopted him. "That is a traditional way Indian people replace a lost loved one," Carson said. "Richard's dad was a Presbyterian minister. He took me as his son because we had served together, his boy and me, and I named my middle son Richard because of him. Richard Spider was a good man. He was older than I was. He got the Bronze Star and a Purple Heart. That is the thing that people who have never been in uniform don't seem to realize, what the real cost of war is. He's not here and I am, but his name lives on with my son."

Because Joseph Medicine Crow was his uncle, Carson went to Vietnam hoping to return a Crow war chief like him. To be named a war chief, Carson needed to do four types of coup: touch an enemy in battle, take an enemy's weapon, lead a war party in which no one gets hurt, and capture an enemy horse. Carson accomplished three of the four coups, but he failed to capture a horse because the Vietcong did not have horses. He did, however, capture four Vietcong elephants loaded with weapons. Too bad, the Crow elders said upon his return home. Elephants are not horses. Although Carson missed out on becoming a Crow war chief, he did receive numerous awards for his military heroism, including the Silver Star, the Bronze Star, two Purple Hearts, and the Vietnamese Gallantry Cross, plus unit citations and campaign ribbons.

Another Cold War veteran with a remarkable service record was Vernon Tsoodle, a member of the Kiowa Nation. The Marine Corps veteran, who died in 2011, served two tours in Korea and two in Vietnam before retiring in 1973 with the rank of master gunnery sergeant (E-9) after thirty years' military service, including his time with the National Guard. Like so many of the Native Americans in the military today, Vernon's ancestors were noted warriors and his family followed in that tradition. The Tsoodles can claim more than thirty men and women who have served in the armed forces since World War II, including Vernon's two sons, a daughter, and three grandchildren.

Vernon earned the Bronze Star during his first tour of duty in the Korean War. The citation reads, "For heroic achievement in connection with operations against an enemy on 28 November 1950. . . . Private First Class Tsoodle's initiative and courageous actions were in keeping with the highest traditions of the United States Naval Service." Vernon says he never saw himself as an Indian. "I was a Marine. Because I was an Indian, however, my fellow Marines throughout my career called me 'Chief.' People often asked me if that offended me. It didn't and it still doesn't. It was never said or meant in a derogatory manner. To them a chief was a leader, so how

Vernon Tsoodle's dance regalia, featuring a Marine medallion on a beaded necklace, beaded pin, blanket, and a gourd rattle made from a Vietnamese hand grenade, all of which reflect his devotion to his culture and to the Marine Corps. Courtesy Vernon Tsoodle.

could it be a bad thing to be compared to? I was pleased because a chief was a great warrior."

Few families—either Indian or non-Indian—can rival the military record of the Emhoolah brothers of the Kiowa Nation. Six saw active duty. A seventh brother tried to enlist but failed the physical exam. Four of the brothers saw combat either in Korea or Vietnam. All the brothers survived, and all graduated from college even though they were raised in a traditional Kiowa-speaking household.

John Emhoolah, the eldest brother, joined the Oklahoma National Guard while in high school. When the Korean War broke out, his unit

John Emhoolah at the Smithsonian symposium "Our Warrior Spirit: Native Americans in the U.S. Military, December 1, 2011. The eldest of six Kiowa brothers who served in the US military, Emhoolah was a forward observer in the 185th Field Artillery, 45th Infantry Division. Courtesy National Museum of the American Indian, Smithsonian Institution. Photo by Ernest Amoroso.

was mobilized. After training in Japan, he formed part of the landing force at Incheon, Korea, and then moved inland to what was known as the MLR—the main line of resistance—where his unit dug bunkers and settled in for the winter. "We were up there from December through April. We had no heat up there. While I was up on that mountain freezing, I did a lot of thinking," he said. "I thought, we don't have that freedom of religion like other people have. We can't celebrate or do religious ceremonies like others, the Catholics, the Methodists, you name it. They get to do what they want, but not we Indians. We can't even use our eagle feathers."

When Emhoolah returned home from the war, he became a member of the American Indian Higher Education Consortium and lobbied for religious freedom. "Here's the problem," he told government officials. "We Indians fought a war. We come back and we still got this suppression of Indian people. We need a way to make it possible for Indian people to have freedom of religion." After other tribal peoples joined the movement, Congress passed the American Indian Religious Freedom Act, which President Jimmy Carter signed into law in 1978. "Now," Emhoolah proudly declares, "we can use our eagle feathers. We can have our powwows. We can sing our songs. So you see, it's all those things. When you go to fight a war, you're not going over there just to kill, you're going over there to make life a little better when you come back. That's the way I looked at it."

LOUIS ADAMS

Cheryl Hughes

Louis "Louie" Adams was a revered Salish elder who lived just north of Missoula on the Flathead Indian Reservation for most of his eighty-two years of life. The only child of Susan Irvine Adams and Lomey Adams, Louie spent his early life in the home of his uncle Sam Resurrection, near Schley, deep in the woods of western Montana. There Louie learned the traditional ways of the Salish people while watching his extended family in "sweats" in lodges just outside their house. He heard the drummings of his family, friends, and neighbors, conducted to commemorate special occasions at powwows—the scalp songs, the war songs, and even the jump songs, which began the new year. Louie

Louis Adams in his navy uniform in 1953 and as a veteran in 2014. Courtesy Cheryl Hughes.

spent much of his early life with "YaYa," his grandmother Caroline Louise Vanderburg.

Louie's uncle Sam Resurrection also had a huge influence on his life. With his unending quest for fairness and equity, Sam exemplified for Louie the undaunted spirit of the Salish. Resurrection, a warrior in his tribe, traveled frequently to Washington, DC, in the early 1900s to advocate for the rights of the Salish as they were forced to merge into white society on the Flathead Reservation.

Louie attended a public school in Arlee, Montana, where he was once struck across the arms for speaking in his native tongue. He remained at this small-town public school a few years, and then his parents sent him to an Indian boarding school in St. Ignatius, but he ran away before the first afternoon was over, returning to his home in Valley Creek, where he attended a country school until the eighth grade.

Adams began to help his parents raise their racehorses (he also became a jockey in the summer) and worked on their ranch near Arlee. Louie's mother was a jockey. His dad was a bronc rider, calf roper, relay race rider, and rancher. Louie followed this lifestyle for several years, but he knew he needed more education and training for economic security in life, so he joined the US Navy in 1951, when he was eighteen, and served on board the USS *Harry E. Hubbard* (DD-748). Besides helping guard the fast carrier task force and repeatedly striking the enemy, the *Hubbard* frequently joined in gun strike missions to bombard coastal rail and communication centers and performed as seagoing artillery to support the advance of land troops. Her bombardment missions were conducted against targets at Yongdae Gap, Wonsan, Songjin, Chingjin, Kyoto, Ohako, Bokukko, Chuminjin, and other enemy strongholds of supply and reinforcement.

Louie spent nearly three years aboard the *Hubbard* in the China Sea. From her decks, he saw a whole new world. He made many friends among the sailors and spent his spare time pursuing his earlier passion as a boxer. As an assembler III during the Korean War, Louie was awarded the Korean Service Medal, the China Service Medal, the United States Service Medal, and the National Defense Services Medal.

After almost four years at sea, he returned to Montana in 1954. Although he remained a reservist in the navy until 1959, he pursued various jobs, married his sweetheart Nadine, and began working at the Diamond Match sawmill in Superior, Montana. After losing nearly all his family possessions in a tragic house fire, Louie and Nadine moved their family back to the Valley Creek area in 1960. Louie then started a career with the Bureau of Indian Affairs and tribal forestry, where he finally retired in 2002. Nadine and Louie had eight children, but they divorced, and he eventually married Gertrude Hanson, a German refugee from the Holocaust. Family was always his priority. At his family's large gatherings in Valley Creek, both Nadine and Gertrude attended. Over the years, Louis Adams became an iconic cultural leader and historian of the Salish people and their land. He represented the Arlee area on the tribal council for more than twenty years and became a beloved symbol of the Salish community. Louie died on April 25, 2016, at his home in Valley Creek.

PASCAL POOLAW

In the Native tribes and nations with a warrior tradition, military societies help keep that tradition alive. One of the most celebrated is the Tonkongo, or Black Leggings Society, of the Kiowa Tribe of Oklahoma. How the society got its name is unknown. Some think it derives from the trail dust that blackened the legs of warriors after a long trek. Others suggest it is in honor of Kiowa warriors who survived an attempt by enemies to defeat them by setting fire to the prairie grasses during a battle. Regardless, the society flourished during the nineteenth century until driven underground around 1890 by the Bureau of Indian Affairs, which sought to eradicate all forms of traditional religion practiced by Native peoples in North America. By 1928, the society had ceased to function. Thirty years later, it was revitalized by Kiowa veterans, including Gus Palmer, who dedicated the revival to the memory of his brother

Lyndreth, who was killed in World War II. "It is a society that never forgets," Lyndreth once said. "We must never ever forget our veterans. We pay honor to the people who made the supreme sacrifice. Their names will never die, never."

Thanks to the efforts of the few surviving society members who taught the songs, dances, and traditions to younger veterans, the Black Leggings Society is now active and vibrant. According to Gus Palmer, who died in November 2006 at age eighty-seven, "The old people said, you younger men are entitled to carry it on. You men today are just like the men in the old days—warriors. You fought for your people."

Membership is restricted to enrolled Kiowas. Members wear black leggings and a red cape, which symbolizes the red cape captured from a Mexican army officer. The society emblem is a curved staff wrapped in otter fur. The society tepee features the battle designs of a famous nineteenth-century war chief on one side and the service crests of today's Kiowa servicemen on the other. It also features the names of the nine Kiowa servicemen killed in combat since World War I.

The society holds mourning feasts, conducts sacred ceremonies, and performs graveside tributes for deceased members. At each biannual ceremony the society provides a meal to all in attendance. Female relatives of society members perform scalp and victory dances using men's lances and feathered headdresses to open the afternoon events, while inside the tepee the men prepare for the five types of dances they will perform. Once a year the society performs the Tsat'hoigya, or Reverse Dance, during which a combat veteran stops the drum and recites a personal battle exploit.

The society's most distinguished member was First Sergeant Pascal Cleatus Poolaw. A veteran of three wars—World War II, Korea, and Vietnam—Sergeant Poolaw is acclaimed as the United States' most decorated "warrior in uniform." He earned forty-two medals, badges, citations, and campaign ribbons, including twenty-two for combat service and thirteen decorations for valor—three Silver Stars, five Bronze Stars, three Purple Hearts (one in each war), three Army Commendation

Medals, and the Distinguished Service Cross. He was also nominated for the Congressional Medal of Honor.

Although Sergeant Poolaw retired in 1962, he reentered the army five years later in an effort to keep his son Lindy from having to go to Vietnam. Another son, Pascal C. Poolaw Jr., had already served in Vietnam, losing a leg in an explosion, and army regulations prohibited two members of the same family from serving in a combat zone without their consent. But he was too late. Upon reaching the point of departure on the West Coast, Sergeant Poolaw discovered that Lindy had left for Vietnam the day before, so he decided to follow him. Having father and son in combat at the same time was nothing new to the Poolaw family. Pascal had served in World War II with his father and two brothers. But this time luck ran out for Pascal. Four months after arriving in Vietnam, he was killed in action while trying to carry a wounded soldier to safety. In a letter to his wife, Irene, shortly before his death, Pascal wrote that he considered his military service more important than his life. Irene echoed that sentiment in her eulogy at his funeral. "He has followed the trail of the great chiefs," she affirmed. "His people hold him in honor and the highest esteem. He has given his life for the people and the country he loved so much." Pascal had four sons. Each entered the army and three served in Vietnam.

Sources

"Anthony T. Kaho'ohanohano." The Hall of Valor Project. Accessed June 10, 2021. https://valor.militarytimes.com/hero/7042.

"Herbert K. Pililaau." The Hall of Valor Project. Accessed June 10, 2021. https://valor.militarytimes.com/hero/1344.

Holm, Tom. *Strong Hearts, Wounded Souls: Native American Veterans of the Vietnam War*. Austin: University of Texas Press, 1996.

"James Elliott Williams." The Hall of Valor Project. Accessed June 11, 2021. https://valor.militarytimes.com/hero/1552.

"Michael Edwin Thornton." The Hall of Valor Project. Accessed June 10, 2021. https://valor.militarytimes.com/hero/2381.

Pearson, Michelle. "Preserve America Youth Summit: Sand Creek Massacre Dedication 2007."

"Roy Perez Benavidez." The Hall of Valor Project. Accessed June 10, 2021. https://valor.militarytimes.com/hero/2809.

Smithsonian National Museum of the American Indian. "Sand Creek Massacre: 13 Memorialization and Healing—Ben Nighthorse Campbell." *YouTube*, 16 October 2014.

Viola, Herman J. *Ben Nighthorse Campbell: An American Warrior.* New York: Orion Books, 1993.

CHAPTER 8

The War on Terror

Since September 11, 2001, when Middle Eastern terrorists captured four airplanes and attacked the Twin Towers in New York City and the Pentagon in Washington, DC, the United States has been engaged in an ongoing series of conflicts in the Middle East, primarily Afghanistan, Iraq, and Syria. These conflicts, however, are unlike any other in America's military history. The enemy is zealous, elusive, and seldom in uniform. More often than not, the enemy arsenal consists of suicide bombers, booby traps, and hidden explosives.

These conflicts threaten to become the longest war in American history, with no end in sight. Even so, American Indian men and women continue to serve in record numbers. Ironically, even though much of the weaponry in use in the Middle East is on the cutting edge of technology—reflecting the computer-driven world of the twenty-first century—the Pentagon again has called upon Native Americans to apply skills honed in another era to solve a modern military problem. Instead of Code Talkers to send secret messages, the US Army now needs trackers who can find an enemy that eludes radar, motion detectors, cameras, and laser technology.

Alarmed at the ease with which enemy fighters were slipping in and out of Afghanistan and Iraq, the Pentagon in early 2007 sent an elite group of well-trained Native American marksmen and trackers to teach their skills to police units in Tajikistan and Uzbekistan, two countries that border Afghanistan.

Known as "Shadow Wolves," the special unit was recruited from several tribes, including the Apache, Blackfeet, Cheyenne, Lakota, Navajo, and Tohono O'odham. Highly skilled in an ancient art and reminiscent of the Apache scouts who helped the US Cavalry capture Geronimo a century earlier, the Shadow Wolves are expert at noticing clues like twigs snapped by a passing person and pieces of fabric or strands of hair snagged on a branch. The professional trackers can tell how long a sliver or crumb of food has lain in the dirt or whether someone has tried to conceal his tracks by strapping pieces of carpet to his shoes.

The Shadow Wolves use the skills that many of them learned as children tracking wild animals while hunting on their reservations or finding livestock that may have wandered away. "Instead of tracking an animal, we now track human beings," said Bryan Nez, a Navajo who was one of the Shadow Wolves. To qualify for the special unit, recruits must be one-quarter Indian.

Typical of the Indian soldiers fighting in the War on Terror is Master Sergeant Johancharles Van "Chuck" Boers, an enrolled Lipan Apache, who retired in 2009 after twenty-six years of military service. From the US government, Chuck received three Purple Hearts and two Bronze Stars for his service. From the Lipan Apaches in December 2007, while he was still on active duty, he was accorded the title of war chief. The tribe's last war chief was Magoosh, who died in 1900.

Chuck's mother is Chiricahua-Lipan Apache and Western Band Cherokee from Oklahoma. His father is a Dutchman who came to the United States from Holland after World War II with his family. While growing up, Chuck learned about Apache culture from his grandfather, and Cherokee culture from his grandmother. Although his mother's family was from Oklahoma and Texas, he grew up primarily in California. "One might think being so far away from our tribal roots that we would lose touch of who we are," Chuck says, "but that was not the case. My grandparents showed and shared with me and my sisters the richness and vibrancy of our culture. Nonetheless, it was not always easy growing up as an Urban Indian, never really quite fitting in the red or white worlds." What stands out for Chuck were the powwows he attended. "My favorite part of the powwow was the Grand Entry when the veterans would bring in the Colors and then afterwards they would do an honor dance. I was

Master sergeant and Lipan Apache war chief Chuck Boers,
bringing in Eagle Staff at the beginning of the powwow,
as befitting a tribal war chief. Courtesy Chuck Boers.

taught that we always welcome home our warriors with songs and
dances, and my thoughts always turned towards my parents, uncles,
and other relatives who had served in the military. I was proud of
them and of the sacrifices that they had made for all of us."

Chuck joined the army in 1982, just after graduating from high
school. The person who recruited him was his mother, Virginia,

a sergeant first class who spent eleven of her twenty years in the army as a recruiter. "I have always looked up to my parents and my other relatives who had served in the military. In fact, our family has served in every war that the United States has had since World War I. We even had family serve as army scouts in the late 1800s. I wouldn't call us patriotic, but we are proud to serve our people and protect our way of life. I knew I wanted to be part of that world. It is part of our culture to be warriors."

Indeed so. His mother, the oldest of five children, had four brothers, and all of them followed her into the army. Three were combat medics and one served in the Air Defense Artillery. One brother served two tours in Vietnam as a special forces medic, followed by a tour in Kuwait during Operation Desert Storm. "Given the family history," she said, "I was proud and pleased that Chuck was continuing our family and tribal tradition—to serve in the military."

Chuck thanks his mother not only for getting him into the army but also for helping him make it through boot camp. As luck would have it, he was assigned to the same camp and same barracks as his mother when she went through basic training at Fort McCullen, Alabama. "When the training got tough, I would tell myself—'If my mom, who is less than five feet tall, could do it, so could I.' My mother not only thought it was cool but that it would also give us a different kind of bond—not only as mother and son, but also as soldiers."

As a combat photographer, Chuck was deployed to all of the US Army's hot spots during the War on Terror—Grenada, Haiti, Bosnia, Kosovo, and the Middle East, including three tours in Iraq. "Everywhere I went," he recalls, "I always ran into other Natives and we would usually all hang out together and tell stories about powwows and stuff like that, but nothing could have prepared me for my fourth tour to the Middle East during Operation Iraqi Freedom. Every Forward Operating Base (FOB) or mission I went on, I would run into another Native. It was something I had never experienced in my whole military career."

One of those warriors in uniform Chuck met in Iraq was Sam Stitt, a Choctaw from Oklahoma serving in the air force. Sam was a military linguist fluent in Arabic with training in Iraqi dialects. At the time, he was assigned to a small team operating in south-central Iraq on a base outside An-Najaf. "I met Chuck when he came to An-Najaf for an anticipated 'action' and higher-ups wanted some pictures," Sam says. Only after working together for several days did they discover their shared Native American heritage. "You don't usually make it a habit to randomly ask people what their ethnicity is," Sam laughs. "Let me tell you, it was quite an experience to run into another Native in the middle of a combat zone. He was down there for a couple of weeks and we would chat for hours about dancing, singing, family, and tribal issues. We talked about hitting the Powwow Highway together when we got home. In such a short amount of time it felt like we had been friends for years."

Like his newfound friend, Sam entered military service because, as a Choctaw, it seemed the thing to do. "Most Choctaw families have some tie to a veteran," Sam says. "It's a tradition of sorts, and when I was young I just assumed that one day I would join. The young kids at the gatherings or powwows look up to the vets and it is something honorable—even if the war itself isn't. That is one reason non-Native vets show up at Native events. They know that they will get the respect they deserve, especially the Vietnam vets. Many of them had it rough fitting back into a society that could be hostile to them at times."

The day before leaving An-Najaf for the anticipated maneuver, Chuck and Sam decided to create a wall mural declaring their tribal affiliations and marking the date and place as a sort of a memento of their meeting. "We used bits of old plaster or some kind of chalky rock from rubble for the drawing," Sam recalled. Then another combat photographer took the picture. "That photo," Sam marvels, "somehow got back stateside and made its way onto the cover of *Indian Country Today*, the May 9, 2004, issue. We were featured on the same page as the Navajo Code Talkers. What an honor!"

That same year, some of those Native American soldiers managed to bring a little piece of real "Indian Country" to Iraq by celebrating the first traditional powwow ever held in a combat zone. The inspiration of Staff Sergeant Debra Kay Mooney, a Choctaw from Idabel, Oklahoma, it was hosted on September 24, 2004, at the Al Taqaddum Air Base near Fallujah by the 120th Engineer Combat Battalion, a National Guard unit based in Okmulgee, Oklahoma. The goal of the powwow was to promote cultural understanding of Native American heritage with fellow soldiers, sailors, and marines, while bringing a piece of home to the many Native Americans serving in Iraq.

One of the eager participants was Chuck Boers, whose presence at the powwow was purely serendipitous. Recently returned from a combat mission and the happy recipient of a four-day pass, he learned of the powwow from a fellow Native soldier. Since the dates for the powwow fell during his four-day leave, he jumped on a convoy going to Al Taqaddum. Although insurgents attacked the convoy, hitting the vehicles with small arms fire and rocket-propelled grenades, the convoy continued without mishap. "I thought to myself

An all-Cherokee drum group played the music at the powwow held in Iraq in 2004. Courtesy Chuck Boers.

I must be nuts trying to go to a powwow in a combat zone," Chuck admits, but he still looked forward to having a great four days.

At Al Taqaddum, Boers met Staff Sergeant Mooney, who welcomed him and introduced him around. "It was a very surrealistic site. Here we were in the middle of a combat zone and a bunch of Natives had gotten together to hold a powwow. Can you imagine that?" Since nothing like that had ever been done before in a combat zone and he was a combat photographer, Boers volunteered to document the historical event. "Debra had dedicated the event to all 'past and present veterans'—so that was the theme for the powwow." "It was a way to honor our fellow warriors," she says. "We all knew this was going to be a very special event and it would be like no other powwow that any of us had ever attended."

Indeed it was—just like "Indian Fair Days back home," Chuck marvels. The powwow featured an honoring ceremony for a fallen warrior. This was Specialist Raymond Brian Estes III, a Ponca, of Charlie Battery, 4th Battalion, 1st Field Artillery. His family had sent over a shawl to be used during the powwow. Debra Mooney placed

Chuck Boers took this group photo of the major participants in the Iraq powwow. Sergeant Debra Mooney is seated at far right. Courtesy Chuck Boers.

The Iraq powwow opened with a salute to
the US flag. Courtesy Chuck Boers.

During the powwow, there was an honor ceremony for
a fallen soldier—Specialist Raymond Bryan Estes III, a
Ponca. His family sent a shawl to be used in the ceremony,
and it was worn by Specialist Leslie Montemayor, a
soldier of Muscogee (Creek) and Seminole heritage, who
danced alone in the arena as everyone paid homage to
their fallen brother warrior. Courtesy Chuck Boers.

the shawl over Specialist Leslie Montemayor, a soldier of Muscogee (Creek) and Seminole heritage. After receiving the shawl, Leslie danced alone in the arena as everyone stood in honor and remembrance of their fallen brother warrior.

"The powwow was a great success," Chuck declares. "I was amazed at how many other Natives made the trip from all over Iraq. Most everyone had heard about the powwow by word of mouth, from a flyer, or in an email. It was just like back home." The powwow ended, however, not with a traditional Native American ceremony but with a military one: the retirement of the colors.

DEBRA KAY MOONEY

Debra Kay Mooney, retired army sergeant first class, takes justifiable pride in having organized the powwow in Iraq. Because nearly 20 percent of the soldiers in her unit boasted American Indian blood, she thought a powwow would boost unit morale and help offset the

From left: Jason Giles; Sergeant First Class Debra Kay Mooney (Choctaw), with the dress she made for the powwow she organized in Iraq; retired master sergeant Chuck Boers (Lipan Apache); Joseph Medicine Crow (Crow); John Emhoolah (Kiowa); and Herman J. Viola. Photograph taken at the National Museum of the American Indian, December 2, 2011. Courtesy US Army.

pangs of homesickness. "We're brought up with powwows," she says. "The beat of the drum is a part of the heartbeat of a Native American." However, the organizers had only a five-week window in which to plan. Dances and events had to be organized and rehearsed. Some Native dress, jewelry, and other essential regalia came from families back home. Others were fashioned from scraps of cloth, trash, and scavenged military gear. The drum came from a discarded 55-gallon oil barrel cut in half, over which canvas taken from a cot was stretched. Metal salvaged from truck doors formed the tomahawks used in a throwing contest. The stickball game featured sticks made from mallets, with the baskets created using standard-issue 5-50 parachute cord.

Despite the challenges, the powwow exceeded expectations. "It gave us a little more pride—a little more heart—not just to get it done, but to get it done right," Debra beams. "We were representing the Oklahoma National Guard. We were representing Oklahoma Native American tribes and pride, and we were representing us individually. It now belongs to our family, to our future. Our children, our grandchildren, our great-grandchildren can say, 'Hey did you hear about the powwow in Iraq in 2004? My ancestors were there.' You know, it's our story and our story belongs to our bloodline now." The story also belongs to the nation as well, because, following the powwow, Sergeant Mooney managed to ship all the regalia to the National Museum of the American Indian, where it resides as a tribute to our nation's Native heritage.

Debra, the first woman in her family to serve in the military, says that even in Iraq she never dwelt much on the fact that she was a woman among mostly male soldiers and marines. "We were all just soldiers." Maybe so, but her soldiers noticed. They changed her name to "Sgt. Mooneye" on her email account.

JOSHUA WHEELER

The first American soldier killed fighting ISIS was Master Sergeant Joshua Wheeler, a Cherokee. Wheeler was a member of the army's elite Delta Force. A secret unit, Delta Force is not officially acknowledged, but it is the army counterpart to navy SEAL teams.

Wheeler died October 22, 2015, while rescuing ISIS prisoners near Hawijah in Northern Iraq. He was thirty-nine years old and the father of four children. American forces were not to engage in combat in

Joshua Wheeler. Courtesy US Army.

Iraq but only provide assistance to Kurdish commandos fighting Islamic State militants. On that fateful day, US soldiers accompanied Kurdish commandos on a helicopter raid to rescue some seventy hostages about to be executed by Islamic State militants. When the attack on the prison where the hostages were held stalled, Sergeant Wheeler responded. "He ran to the sound of the guns," a Defense Department official reported. "Obviously, we're very saddened that he lost his life," he said, adding, "I'm immensely proud of this young man." The mission was a success and the hostages were freed. The only rescuer who died was Sergeant Wheeler. A veteran of fourteen deployments to Iraq and Afghanistan, he had earned mulitple honors, including four Bronze Stars with the letter V, awarded for valor in combat, and seven Bronze Stars awarded for heroic or meritorious service in a combat zone. Wheeler's death shocked his tight-knit family, few of whom knew the dangerous life he led. "I really thought my brother was invincible," said Tatira Wade, Wheeler's sister, "He was like my Superman. Memorial Day has a whole new meaning for me now."

Sources

Gibson, Daniel. "Desert Thunder: Powwow in Iraq." *Native Peoples Magazine*, March/April 2005.

Harris, Alexandra N., and Mark G. Hirsch. *Why We Serve: Native Americans in the United States Armed Forces.* Washington, DC: National Museum of the American Indian, 2020.

Lamothe, Dan. "A Memorial Day without Joshua Wheeler, the Elite Delta Force Soldier Killed Fighting ISIS." *Washington Post*, May 28, 2016.

Viola, Herman J. *Warriors in Uniform.* Washington, DC: National Geographic Society, 2008.

Zotigh, Dennis. "A Tradition of Service: Master Sergeant and Lipan Apache War Chief Chuck Boers." *Smithsonian Voices*, November 10, 2019. Smithsonianmag.com.

CHAPTER 9

Women Warriors

Where once being a warrior was considered a man's job, today it is a vocation open to Native American women as well, as evidenced by Choctaw sergeant Debra Kay Mooney, who wrote the foreword to this book, and by the tragic story of Private First Class Lori Ann Piestewa, a Hopi who died in Iraq in 2003. Lori received national recognition as the first American Indian woman service member ever killed in combat. Wayne Taylor, the tribal chair, said that the most frequently asked question on the Hopi reservation was "Why did Lori join the Army?" Perhaps it was because of the family's military legacy—her father had served in Vietnam and her grandfather in World War II. Or it may have been her ROTC training in high school. "Whatever the reason," Chairman Taylor said, "the question should not be why did she join, but rather, why is it strange for her not to?"

Besides being the first Native woman service member to die in combat, Lori now has another claim to fame. The twenty-three-year-old mother of two did not move mountains, but she did change a mountain's name. "Squaw Peak," the former offensive and controversial name of a mountain summit near Phoenix, Arizona, is now "Piestewa Peak" in her honor.

In truth, Native American women had little opportunity to serve in our nation's armed forces until World War II, but there were exceptions, such as the Oneida woman Tyonajanegen. As noted in chapter 1, she accompanied her husband in battle during the American Revolution and, when he was wounded, loaded his musket for him so he could continue fighting. Another, better-known Native American heroine is Sacagawea, the Shoshone woman who accompanied the Lewis and Clark expedition at the opening of the nineteenth century. Serving as guide and interpreter for the explorers, she provided a presence—that of a woman with a child among armed men—which was crucial to the success of the military and exploratory mission, because it indicated to tribal peoples encountered along their journey to the Pacific Ocean that the explorers had peaceful, not warlike, intent.

LORI ANN PIESTEWA

Private First Class Lori Ann Piestewa, a Hopi mother of two, was the first American Indian woman ever to die in combat while serving in the US armed forces. A member of the Quarter Master Corps, she died on March 23, 2003, during the Iraq War. As one of Lori's childhood friends remembers, "We grew up together in Tuba City on the Navajo Reservation that shares a border with the Hopi Reserva-

Lori Ann Piestewa. Courtesy Piestewa family.

tion. Pie is the name friends use when referring to the Piestewa family. To us, she was Lori Pie, and she had many friends because she had a big heart and friendly spirit. She was one person who always had a huge smile and friendly words for you. Lori was very active in high school. She was always busy preparing herself for up-and-coming events, working out, running, practicing. She seemed to be more competitive with herself than with anyone else, yet always encouraging her fellow teammates along the way. We all knew she was the best—so athletic. But her humble attitude was always present. She never claimed to be 'The Best,' never boasted about herself. So, naturally, when a female is so strong and athletic, boys always want to see just how strong she is, so they have boys versus girls competitions. Her older brothers were also athletic and they knew her strength. They always warned the boys that 'she's tough and good luck.' Her parents always called her 'a tough cookie.' When it came to these friendly competitions, girls on the Rez have phrases like 'Don't be such a Girl' or 'Don't cry like a Girl,' which means don't be so sensitive, whine around, or expect someone to do it for you, toughen up! If you 'want it' you have to be willing to put in the work. And Lori did. It has been definitely nice to hear her squad, platoon, and army friends describing her strengths, because that's what she always exuded. It's what her parents encouraged, it's what she got from her culture, and it was what she learned from her family—strength. A strong woman. One who knows when to nurture and one who protects. A warrior."

Most of the Native women who participated in various military conflicts prior to World II were nurses. For example, four Native American Catholic Sisters from Fort Berthold, South Dakota, worked for the War Department during the Spanish-American War. One of them, Sister Anthony, died of disease in Cuba and was buried with full military honors. During World War I, fourteen Native American women served as members of the Army Nurse Corps, two of them overseas.

According to the Women in Military Service for America Memorial Foundation, about eight hundred Native women served in the US military during World War II, primarily in the Women's Army Corps (WAC) and in the navy reserve known as Women Accepted for Volunteer Emergency Service (WAVES). One of these women, Minnie Spotted Wolf of the Blackfeet Nation, is recognized as the first Native woman to join the Marine Corps. Before enrolling in the Corps in 1943, Minnie had worked on her father's ranch in Butte, Montana, doing such heavy-duty chores as cutting fence posts, driving a two-ton truck, and breaking horses. Her comment after marine boot camp was "Hard but not too hard." Minnie served in the Marine Corps for four years as a heavy-equipment operator. After her discharge, she received a college degree in education and taught high school for twenty-nine years.

In addition to serving in the military, thousands of Native women supported the troops during both world wars by working in

war-related industries and through efforts such as Red Cross clothing drives. After every war, Native women have also cared for the
physically and mentally wounded after they come home. "Whether
providing support in the form of supplies and healing or serving as
leaders and warriors in their own right, Native women have always
played critical military roles for their tribal nations and the United
States," as explained in *Why They Serve,* published by the National
Museum of the American Indian (2020). Nonetheless, regardless of
how they have served their communities and country, their stories
are rarely told in the history books. "In part, this omission could be
because those histories typically focus on battles. Yet throughout the
more than two centuries of U.S. military history, Native women are
at the center of the story, not a marginal part of the story."

On and off the battlefield, Native women have served in every
branch of the US armed forces and, just like other women veterans,
they joined for a variety of reasons and they shared many of the same
struggles. That is why the goal of acknowledging all Native warriors
in uniform—male and female—for their service was one of the driving forces behind the National Native American Veterans Memorial,
dedicated in Washington, DC, on November 11, 2020.

One of those women warriors is Mitchelene BigMan (Crow and
Hidatsa), who served on the advisory board for the memorial's creation. Mitchelene, who enlisted in the US Army in 1987, served as a
diesel mechanic, attaining the rank of sergeant first class. Deployed
twice during Operation Iraqi Freedom in Balad, Iraq, she knew from
personal experience that Indigenous servicewomen often do not
get credit for their work and feel they have to try harder to prove
themselves. "Our women were the first to volunteer for the craziest
missions knowing we may not make it home," she says. "When we
had to go to a village, I'd go in and I'd have to pretend that I was not
scared, even though I was terrified."

"When Lori Piestewa became the first Native service woman to
die in combat, I just cried," BigMan admits. "It hit home. It could

have been me. She made the ultimate sacrifice. She kissed her kids goodbye and didn't come home. I listened to flute music and burned sage. As a soldier, we are trained not to think we are women. Women leaders were often criticized that we wear our heart on our stripes." She cared for those under her command. "Those soldiers relied on me, expected that I would bring them home safe." But then, she says, "if I am a soldier, treat me like one. Treat me as a comrade." But that did not often happen, because she is a woman.

While many tribes acknowledge and respect their women veterans, BigMan says that after her retirement in 2009, even her own people did not recognize what she had done. And so she founded Native American Women Warriors (NAWW), the first all-female Native American color guard, to help raise awareness of the contributions made by women veterans. Her organization also helps Native veterans find resources in employment and educational opportunities and provides some emergency funds to pay for the cost of necessities such as rent, utilities, and food.

When Native American Women Warriors was given the opportunity to lead at BigMan's own tribe's annual powwow celebration, they were met with resistance from some of her own tribal members. "They said we weren't supposed to march in front." That has now changed. The women, in their bright red, white, or blue jingle dresses decorated with metal cones have since appeared in color guards at various powwows, President Obama's inaugural parade in 2013, the Native Nations Inaugural Ball at the National Museum of the American Indian in 2017, and the Parade Across America, part of the 2021 presidential inauguration.

The original jingle dress of red, white, blue, and Indian pink that BigMan designed is currently in the National Museum of the American Indian. It's colors, she notes, reflect the patriotism of both non-Native and Native American veterans. The red color signifies the blood that was shed for the United States; the blue signifies their valor and courage as warriors.

Native American Women Warriors Honor Guard,
Denver, 2016. Courtesy Mitchelene BigMan.

As BigMan explains, the jingle dance is a "dance of healing. We are dancing for all veterans who have passed. Some tribes regard the jingle dance as a healing rite traditionally performed by women. The members of the NAWW perform the dance to heal from their own injuries that cut deep, and they dance for others, such as Lori Piestewa, who loved the dances of her Hopi people."

The mission statement of NAWW reads: "To establish recognition for all women veterans, especially of Native American descent, and their contribution to the military and the United States of America." BigMan says membership in NAWW is growing and with that growth comes more appreciation for the services of Native American women veterans. "Yet, there will always be another purpose for the organization. If we can assist at least one woman, we've achieved our goal."

JAMIE FOX

Ellen Baumler

Jamie Fox (Gros Ventre and Métis) grew up in a close-knit community in the southern portion of the Fort Belknap Reservation in northern Montana. She remembers a wonderful childhood, playing outside in the creeks and appreciating the beauty of the landscape. But, she explains, despite her pastoral surroundings, there was significant noise pollution from nearby Malmstrom and Ellsworth air force bases. Military aircraft typically practice over reservation lands, and Jamie became fascinated with the heavy aircraft that maneuvered across the sky. The B-1s, F-16s, and

Jamie Fox. Courtesy Jamie Fox.

KC-10s thundering low overhead inspired her to aim for a career in aviation, and her father, also an aviation enthusiast, encouraged her interest.

As in many Native American families, Jamie's relatives carried a long and rich tradition of military service. Because both her grandfathers were World War II veterans and numerous uncles and aunts had served during the wars in Korea, Vietnam, and the Persian Gulf, military service seemed a logical decision for her, but not at first. As a seventeen-year-old high school senior thinking ahead to college, Jamie in 2007 applied to and was accepted at Embry-Riddle Aeronautical University. She still cherishes that acceptance letter, but anticipating the potential expense and unwilling to burden her parents,

Jamie opted to put off college and enlist in the air force so she could later pay her own way.

After enlisting, Jamie persevered for the many months it took her to finally get the assignment she wanted. Twice deployed to the Middle East, she served until 2017 as one of few women trained in heavy-aircraft maintenance tasked with keeping planes mission ready. Confident in her abilities and highly skilled at her job, she was honored as Airman of the Month and Airman of the Quarter. As a crew chief, she practically held the lives of those who flew in those planes in her hands.

Today, American Indian men and women like Jamie continue to serve and honor their warrior cultures. Like other Native veterans, Jamie considers military service a high honor and the extension of the traditional warrior society into which she was born. During a visit home to Fort Belknap following her first deployment, Jamie's community ceremoniously paid her tribute with an eagle feather, a high honor. Her mother was equally honored with a star quilt. Jamie explains that worry for a child in service makes a mother a warrior, too.

Besides military service, Jamie also values music. Jamie's musically talented family has preserved their rich traditions, steeped in Celtic, French, and Native American cultures. As a youngster of ten, Jamie learned to play the fiddle. With her father and siblings, her family has shared their cultural songs and step dances widely. When she enlisted, Jamie took her fiddle with her. Later, after her military service, her cultural heritage helped her through the difficult transition back to civilian life. Today, Jamie is a highly acclaimed Métis master fiddler who performs and teaches her craft. Her military service is part of who she is and, along with her art, she celebrates it. "I wish that more veterans would share their stories," she says, "and celebrate what will always be a big part of their life."

SOPHIE DENET BIA YAZZIE

Ellen Baumler

Sophie Denet Bia Yazzie was born into the Kinyaa'áanii (Towering House) clan of the Navajo Nation in 1914. Her birth name was Awee Yahtzi. When her father died, she took the name of her stepfather, Dine Bia. Her life was not so remarkable, but her quiet, lifelong dedication and patriotism made her a role model and a respected Navajo warrior and matriarch.

Sophie grew up herding sheep—important for the wool used by acclaimed Navajo weavers—and farming in the shadows of the beautiful Canyon del Muerto in Canyon de Chelly (pronounced *de Shay*). Canyon de Chelly is a National Monument in the Four Corners region of Arizona, near the New Mexico border on the Navajo Reservation.

Sophie loved her sheep and the patient little donkeys that stood guard over them. She and her sister slept among them in the summers and played hide-and-seek in the canyon's rocky landscape where Native people have made their homes for five thousand years. Sophie loved the freedom to go where she liked.

Most Navajo children went to boarding schools, where they lived during the school year and sometimes year-round, never seeing their families for months, sometimes years. Sophie was lucky to live near her school in Chinle, Arizona, where she spent part of the year. When she was ready for high school,

Sophie Denet Bia Yazzie, during World War II. Courtesy Kathleen-Phil Lampert.

Sophie attended the Wingate Boarding School across the border in New Mexico, where she graduated in a class of thirty-four in 1934.

After high school, Sophie worked as a hostess and cook in a restaurant. She and others of the Navajo Nation paid close attention to the national news. Even before the Japanese bombed Pearl Harbor in 1941, the Navajo Tribal Council promised allegiance to the United States and to help defend the country.

When the United States entered World War II, Sophie wanted to follow other Navajos and join the marines to become a Code Talker. She tried to enlist, but women were not allowed to become Code Talkers or marines. Instead, she joined the Women's Army Air Corps (WAAC) in January 1943, when she was twenty-eight years old. Besides nursing, WAAC was the only branch of the service at the time that allowed women. WAAC is also said to have stood for "Women's Auxiliary Army Corps." WAAC was a reserve group, designed to serve as backup to the regular army. Sophie was assigned the status of "aviation cadet," which did not imply pilot training but rather any number of support services. As the war progressed, women were needed and on July 1, 1943, the WAAC became the Women's Army Corps (WAC), a regular active-duty unit.

Many women like Sophie on active duty served their country in the United States. After basic training at Daytona Beach, Florida, and advanced individual training (AIT) as a cook, she served at Foster Air Force Base in Victoria, Texas, until her honorable discharge in 1945. At Foster AFB, she cooked for young men training to become fighter pilots. She was a Grade 4 technician sergeant and made a salary of $78 a month.

After her discharge, Sophie came back to the Navajo Nation and went to work as assistant head cook at Wingate Boarding School, her alma mater. There she met her husband, Jordan B. Yazzie, who worked in the school's warehouse maintenance department. Sophie and Jordan raised two daughters and two sons. Jordan died in 1979, and Sophie retired from the school in the mid-1980s when she returned to her beloved canyon and a simpler lifestyle. Into her nineties, Sophie farmed and herded sheep. According to her daughter, Sophie "walked up and down the canyon like a mountain goat, carrying groceries and fruits." She grew all kinds of vegetables, as well as peach and other fruit trees.

Sophie was always proud of her military service, but it was during her retirement that her patriotism came to the forefront. In 2013 and 2014, she participated in the Coalition for American Indian Veterans of Southern Arizona. In 2014, she flew with other veterans to Washington, DC, where she was inducted into the Women in Military Service for America at the Women's Memorial Library.

Sophie Denet Bia Yazzie in 2018. Photo courtesy of Kathleen-Phil Lampert.

In 2016, she was the special guest in the commander's tent at the Davis Monthan Air Force Base in Tucson, Arizona. In 2015, 2016, and 2017, she was honored as Arizona's oldest female World War II veteran at the Iwo Jima Flag Raising Parade in Sacaton, Arizona. She also served several times as grand marshal at the parade. When she died at her daughter's home in Tucson on January 25, 2020, at age 105, she was one of the nation's oldest living World War II veterans. Sophie's medals and decorations include the Women's Army Corps Service Medal, American Campaign Medal, World War II Victory Medal, and Navajo Nation Service Medal.

Sources

Bolen, Ann. "Women Warriors: Fighting on Many Fronts for the Right to Serve." *American Indian* 21, no. 3 (Fall 2020).

Harris, Alexandra N., and Mark G. Hirsch. *Why We Serve: Native Americans in the United States Armed Forces*. Washington, DC: National Museum of the American Indian, 2020.

Viola, Herman J. *Warriors in Uniform*. Washington, DC: National Geographic Society, 2008.

CHAPTER 10

Fallen Warriors

Sadly, not all welcome-home celebrations for veterans are joyous occasions like the one for Joseph Medicine Crow. For some, it is like the solemn ceremony held in February 2006 at the Pine Ridge Reservation town of Kyle, South Dakota, that honored Marine Corporal Brett L. Lundstrom, the first Oglala Lakota fatality of Operation Iraqi Freedom. The ceremony began as a procession consisting of a hearse, two vans carrying twelve Marines in dress uniforms, and a police escort that wound its way to the middle of the two million–acre reservation, the poorest county in the United States. The procession grew and grew as cars and pickup trucks parked along the road took their places at the end of the line.

The procession eventually stopped where a dozen or so horsemen, several wearing eagle feather warbonnets, waited at the side of the road with a small, empty horse-drawn wagon. After lifting the flag-draped casket from the hearse and placing it gently on the bed of the old wagon, the marines stood at attention in their spotless dress-blue uniforms, white gloves, and ebony shoes.

"Unkiyapo," one of the riders said. "Let's go." Together they walked, the marines in crisp formation behind the riders. The saddle of the last horse was empty.

Upon reaching the Little Wound High School, the marines carried the flag-draped casket into the gymnasium and placed it before a 30-foot-tall tepee at one end of the hardwood floor. Then, beginning a rotation that would last for two days and nights, two Marines positioned themselves at opposite ends of the open casket.

Seated in the gymnasium were friends and relatives of Lundstrom's family as well as numerous Lakota veterans who had come to honor the fallen warrior. Most of the veterans were wearing their service caps and uniforms, many of them emblazoned with unit patches, ribbons, and medals. Tucked into some of the caps was a single eagle feather.

Like Joseph Medicine Crow, Brett Lundstrom boasted a distinguished warrior heritage. Ironically, his ancestors often earned their warrior honors fighting the Crows, once the mortal enemies of the Lakotas. One of his distant relatives was Iron Hail, also known as Dewey Beard, who fought against Custer in the Battle of the Little Bighorn. Another ancestor was the great Lakota leader Red Cloud. No matter. Now the Crows and Lakotas are on the same side. One of Brett's uncles was killed at the Battle of the Bulge during World War II. Another uncle died in Korea. His father, Ed Lundstrom, a career marine, had retired recently as a major. Brett served three months in Afghanistan in 2004 before going to Iraq, where he was killed January 7, 2006, by small-arms fire in Fallujah. Corporal Lundstrom was twenty-two.

Upon their return from military service, Lakota warriors receive an eagle feather, the tribe's highest honor. If the recipient was injured in combat, the feather might have a red stain. As John Around Him, who emceed the ceremony, explained, "Brett earns the American flag from his government. From his people, he earns the eagle feather."

That night Corporal Lundstrom, who had never lived on the reservation—because his father was stationed elsewhere during his military career—was given a new name by his great-uncle Birgil Kills Straight. "Before he enters the spirit world, it's important for him to have an Indian name, because that's how the ancestors will know him," Kills Straight explained. "After the ceremony, his spirit ancestors will visit the dead Marine inside the tepee. That is why he needs a new name, so the spirits will know who he is, and the name I am giving him is Wanbli Isnala, Lone Eagle." With that, Birgil Kills Straight took the eagle feather, walked to the open casket, and placed it on Brett's chest. "He, alone, above everything else, is an eagle," Kills

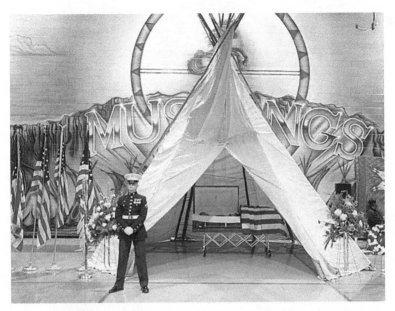

Honor guard for Marine Corporal Brett Lundstrom at his wake in the Little Wound High School gymnasium on the Pine Ridge Reservation, January 2006. Todd Heisler/*Rocky Mountain News*/Polaris.

Straight said. "He will fly to the highest reaches of the universe. He may bring back news to us in our dreams." Kills Straight then told the hushed onlookers about Lundstrom's warrior ancestors. "The blood of these people you've probably never heard of runs in Brett's blood. This is who Brett is. He is a warrior."

As the Lakota drummers and singers began their warrior songs, John Around Him again took the microphone: "This ceremony will continue on into the night," he said, "because in the past, in our history with our great warriors, and how they defended our land, their culture and their way of life—it passes on, generation after generation. These veterans, they love us. They care for us." Then, in concluding his remarks, he said, "To all the veterans who are here tonight, welcome home." Then, looking at the dead marine with an eagle feather on his chest, he said again, "Welcome home."

Sources

Sheeler, Jim. "Wake for an Indian Warrior." *(Denver) Rocky Mountain News*, January 21, 2006.

Viola, Herman J. *Warriors in Uniform*. Washington, DC: National Geographic Society, 2008.

Conclusion

National Native American Veterans Memorial

On November 11, 2020, the National Native American Veterans Memorial was dedicated on the grounds of the National Museum of the American Indian. According to the authorizing legislation, enacted in December 2013, the goal of the memorial is to give "all Americans the opportunity to learn of the proud and courageous tradition of service of Native Americans in the Armed Forces of the United States." This sentiment was echoed at the dedication by Kevin Gover, director of the museum, who declared: "The significance of a Native American veterans' memorial on the National Mall is obvious. Now the world will learn that these people who had been so terribly wronged by our country were nevertheless patriots who believed in the promise of the United States. The memorial will give affirmation to the patriotic contributions of Native American veterans by the federal government as a whole and by the Smithsonian Institution in particular."

Getting the $15 million memorial built was no easy task. Congress authorized the memorial but provided no funds for its construction, so fundraising was a paramount necessity. It was also crucial to obtain the appropriate guidance from those whom the memorial would honor. Accordingly, the museum formed an advisory committee of distinguished Native American veterans and family members from across the nation. Chaired by former senator Ben Nighthorse Campbell, a Northern Cheyenne, and Jefferson Keel, lieutenant governor of the Chickasaw Nation, the committee represented all branches of the armed forces and several eras of service, from the Korean War to the present.

Private First Class Harvey Pratt, US Marine Corps,
Da Nang, Vietnam. Courtesy Gina Pratt.

Assisted by the advisory committee, members of the museum staff spent the better part of two years seeking the advice and opinions of the Indian community. They held thirty-five consultations in sixteen states and the District of Columbia. All told, the staff met with some twelve hundred people who shared their thoughts, hopes, and concerns about the proposed memorial. The response was universal acclaim. In fact, a number of the Native veterans, when they expressed their support for the memorial, became emotional as they spoke.

One of the most poignant and powerful statements of the need for and value of the proposed memorial was provided by a Kiowa soldier who had served a tour in Afghanistan. A colonel in the US Army, she described an encounter she had with Afghan villagers. Upon meeting the dark-skinned woman, they asked about her ethnicity. When her interpreter told them she was an Indian, they immediately began shouting, "India! India!" No, she told her interpreter, not India. "Tell them I am an American Indian." They still failed to understand until the interpreter explained that she was a "Red American." After briefly chatting among themselves, one of the villagers then said that they were still puzzled. "How can you be a Red American?" he asked. "We heard that the Americans had killed all their Red People." As she recalled that dramatic moment, the colonel began crying. "That is why this memorial is so important," she told the museum staff. "The memorial will educate other cultures, other people around the globe who will visit the memorial and learn that we Indian people are still here."

The consultation findings were clear. The memorial had to honor the service of *all* Native American veterans—American Indian, Alaska Native, and Native Hawaiian men and women from all branches of the United States armed forces—and it had to be timeless, honoring past, present, and future military service. Although the attendees at the consultations accepted the fact that the memorial had to have space enough to accommodate large gatherings and ceremonies, they expressed the hope that there could also be a quiet area for private, spiritual reflection, a place of healing for veterans, their families, and returning service members.

Following the consultations, the museum opened a design competition that produced 120 design proposals from across the world. To judge the proposals, the museum appointed an eight-member jury consisting of distinguished artists, historians, cultural experts, and veterans. Their unanimous choice was *Warriors' Circle of Honor*, by Harvey Pratt, a member of the Cheyenne and Arapaho Tribes of Oklahoma and a Southern Cheyenne peace chief.

Pratt's design features a semi-enclosed circular space with a vertical, water-filled stainless-steel circle atop a low, cylindrical stone drum that gently pulses ripples from its center. At the base of the circle a flame can be lit during ceremonies and special gatherings. On a nearby stone wall are five circular seals, one for each of the five branches of the armed forces of the United States. The circular gathering area has points of entry at the four cardinal directions and benches for those who wish to spend time in contemplation or prayer. In addition, there are four lances to which veterans, family members, tribal leaders, and others can tie cloths for prayers and healing. Another distinguishing feature is a continuous loop of music of thirteen Native American veteran songs from the Ojibwe, Menominee, Blackfeet, Ho-Chunk, Kiowa, and Lakota Nations.

Both simple and powerful, the memorial evokes the concept of the sacred circle of time and life that is at the core of Native American cultures. As the selection committee noted, the design's "concept of the circular nature of life makes individual veteran experiences and stories part of a collective unified experience."

Harvey Pratt, a Marine Corps veteran who saw service in Vietnam, says the design for the National Native American Veterans Memorial came to him in a dream. "A lot of things come to me in dreams," he explains. "I wake up early in the morning, think about it, work it through my mind, so I already have an idea of what to do, without having to start working through it. It was my experience of a lifetime—the brain just put it all together for me—what I was taught, what I learned on my own, what I learned from other people."

The primary challenge of the design, Pratt admits, was trying to find common threads among more than 573 known North American tribes, each of which is unique. "I've been with a lot of tribes in ceremonies, and I thought, you know, the way you touch everybody is through tradition and ceremonies. Most ceremonies involve the elements—water, fire, the earth, and the air. And they are all sacred. And we know the directions are sacred. They say power comes from these different directions. Some tribes only recognize four. A lot of tribes recognize six directions. Some tribes recognize seven." Each has a different meaning and color, from the red of the Southwest, "where the creator comes from," to the yellow of the Northwest, "for Mother Earth, who gives us the plants, the animals, the water, the vegetation. And that is where we learn a lot of our traditions."

As Pratt points out, "The design employs water, fire, an eagle feather, a drum, cardinal points, a dedicated pathway, and a lesson from Pratt's grandfather. I remember my grandfather saying, 'Wear a circle, people. We go in a circle, and come back to ourselves, then go back around it.' Path of life—the Plains people called it the 'red road.'

Artistic rendering of the National Native American
Veterans Memorial. Harvey Pratt is depicted, seated
facing the Circle of Honor. Courtesy Skyline Ink.

In order to stay in harmony, you have to walk the red road. Sometimes you will get out, and the red road pulls you back to the middle. You might drift out a little bit and then come back in. So, I thought, the design would need a pathway. We will call it the path of life until you get into the area where the directions are, and you come inside where the drum is. Then you come into harmony with all of those things."

For Pratt, nature provided a special omen signifying that the spirit world approved his design. The day he and staff examined the museum grounds, a red-tailed hawk landed on the exact spot Harvey had selected for the memorial. "Look at him," Harvey exclaimed, "he's dancing. He's dancing around where we chose our site." Then the hawk flew up and landed in a tree above the proposed Path of Life and remained there for an hour. "He stayed there for an hour while we walked around and talked about it. And everybody said, 'That's a great sign,'" Pratt said. Indeed it was. His great-great-grandfather's Indian name was Red-Tailed Hawk and it is the Indian name of his brother Charles. "My ancestors came down here to approve of this," Harvey marvels, "and now that hawk shows up all the time."

Like many Native American veterans, Harvey is often asked, Why do Indians fight for this country, when it has treated Native people so badly? "I say there are a couple of reasons. Foremost, we are a warrior society, a warrior culture. I was raised that way. You have to prepare yourself, be brave and not cry. You don't cry because you got hurt. You cry because your heart is broken, because you lost somebody. You learn to suck it up. You suffer in silence. The other thing is the Americas were like the Garden of Eden—nothing here but animals. And all of a sudden, man and woman showed up, and the creator gave the Americas to the Indians. So this land is Indian Country. It is always Indian Country, regardless of who owns it. That's what we fight for. Our blood is spilt all over this North American continent. Now our blood is spilt all over the world, defending this country. That's why we fight for this land and why we fight for that flag. Indian people say things happened to us in the past. But this is still our land, and we fight for it. We fight for this country, and it is my hope that the memorial will inspire visitors to learn more about the great legacy of Indigenous servicemen and servicewomen to this country and shed light on some of the lesser known stories of Native Americans—stories that will move and inspire visitors. I want it to be a place where you are comforted, you are healed, and you're empowered. That's what I think it's going to be. It's going to be a powerful place. It will be timeless. The circle is timeless." Although the memorial is for Native American veterans, Pratt "invites all other veterans to come and be there with us."

HARVEY PRATT

Cheryl Hughes

Harvey Pratt was born in 1941 into a traditional Cheyenne family in El Reno, Oklahoma. He was a veil baby, meaning that the membranes that covered his fetus in utero remained at birth. His family considered that condition significant, a sign that he would become an important tribal member, probably a chief, so they gave him the name Vehunkis, meaning "going to be chief."

Harvey, the sixth of seven children, grew up with a deep connection to his rich heritage and culture as a member of both the Southern Cheyenne and Arapaho tribes. Because his father, Oscar Noble Pratt, who was Arapaho, died when Harvey was nine, he was raised primarily as a Cheyenne by his mother, Anna Guerrier Pratt, who had Cheyenne, Sioux, French, and English heritage. Harvey's maternal grandfather and his mother's aunt also played significant roles in his traditional upbringing. From them he learned the importance of protecting and defending home, family, tribe, and land, and his grandfather schooled him and his siblings in hunting and gathering food in the wild.

Art has defined much of Harvey's life. Since the family had little money to buy toys, he and his siblings made their own toys out of clay their grandfather gave them. Harvey also found encouragement from several teachers who praised his artistic creations. In addition, he found inspiration from his older brother, Charlie Pratt, who eventually became an award-winning Native American sculptor and metalsmith.

When Harvey entered high school in the late 1950s, prejudice against American Indians was pervasive. Like many other Native Americans, he suffered racial slurs and threats. "People would say, You're just Indians. You're not going to amount to anything." As a result of this abusive treatment, his mother sent him to St. Patrick's Mission and Boarding School in Anadarko, Oklahoma, where he could live according to his cultural upbringing. He graduated in 1961.

The memories of that childhood racism continue to haunt him. "It always just pissed me off," he admits. "I thought, you know what, I'm never gonna let that stop me. I'm going to try to be the best I can at whatever I do. I'm not gonna let someone stop me."

Harvey's years in the early sixties were full of challenges, starting with his higher education at Central State College (now the University of Central Oklahoma), in Edmond and continuing on a tour of duty with the US Marines from 1962 to 1965. He served in the Third Marine Division as a military policeman in Okinawa and then on a security and air rescue detail with Charlie Company, Third Recon Battalion, in Da Nang, Vietnam.

When Harvey returned home, the Cheyenne Tribe honored him for his service with a traditional ceremony for warriors. "That's what Indians do," he is proud to say. "We tell our war stories. We expect our veterans to tell us what they did to defend our family, our village, our country. It's therapy. Indians have been treating PTSD for hundreds of years. We do a ceremony to clean and purify veterans so that they feel better."

Upon his return from Vietnam, Harvey reentered Central State College as an art major, but after one of his commercial art professors dismissed his artistic talent, he left the school. In 1965 he joined the Midwest City Police Department, and there he began to build a solid future in law enforcement. He realized the field was changing, and he seized the opportunity to be part of that change. "I really wanted to work in a broader horizon," he says. "I had just started doing some forensic art and I was getting calls from other police departments asking for help with witness description drawings and then I heard about this degree at Oklahoma State University, Oklahoma City."

The associate degree Pratt received from OSU-OKC in 1972 and his graduation from the FBI National Academy opened new doors for his future. He joined the Oklahoma State Bureau of Investigation, where he used his artistic talent to create a new technique for soft-tissue reconstruction, which enabled him to become one of the nation's leading forensic artists. As a result, he has participated in several of the most famous criminal investigations done in the United States over the past fifty years, including the 1977 Oklahoma Girl Scout murders, the 1978 Oklahoma City Sirloin Stockade slayings, and the 1980–81 Interstate Highway 5 murders in Washington, Oregon, and California. Pratt also worked on the investigations of the 1993 World Trade Center Bombing in New York City and the 1995 bombing of the Alfred P. Murrah Federal Building in Oklahoma City. In recognition of his stellar work, Pratt was inducted into the Oklahoma Law Enforcement Hall of Fame and into the Oklahoma Military Hall of Fame. He also chairs the Indian Arts and Crafts Board in the US Department of the Interior.

Harvey Pratt and Herman J. Viola at the groundbreaking
for the National Native American Veterans Memorial,
September 21, 2019. Courtesy Gina Pratt.

Although he retired in 2017, Harvey is still considered one of the leading experts in his field. He is also a leader in his tribe. In 1996 he was accepted into the Southern Cheyenne Chiefs Lodge as one of their traditional peace chiefs and given the name White Thunder. The following year he was named Outstanding Southern Cheyenne.

For many years he had won accolades in art circles and law enforcement across the United States and had earned renown for telling the stories and sharing the art and religion of Native American people.

Still, when encouraged to enter the design competition for the National Native American Veterans Memorial, Harvey hesitated. He said he had to dream about it. The result of that dream is the world-acclaimed memorial dedicated on November 11, 2020.

For Harvey himself it was a monumental experience, he admits. He credits his experiences as an American Indian, an artist, a law enforcement officer, and a veteran, coupled with his lifetime of Native understanding, that enabled him to create this epitome of artistic excellence. The *Warriors' Circle of Honor*, he believes and hopes, "will ensure that the memorial touches everyone with tradition and ceremonies."

Sources

Gover, Kevin. "A New Memorial Honors the Military Services of Native Americans." *Washington Post*, November 11, 2020.

Stoffer, Jeff. "Harvey Pratt's Path of Life." *American Legion Magazine*, October 20, 2020.

Afterword

The warrior spirit of the American Indian veterans and their remarkable contribution to the armed forces of the United States is largely unknown to the world outside Indian Country. I became aware of this only through my work at the Smithsonian Institution as director of the National Anthropological Archives, which has custody of one of the largest and finest collections of American Indian documents, photographs, and art in the United States. Upon becoming director in 1972, I initiated a program to encourage reservation Indians to become tribal archivists, librarians, and historians. As a result, I befriended dozens of Indian men and women who shared my interest in collecting and preserving Native American oral history. They not only shared their stories with me but also gave me permission to share them with others.

One of these friends was Wolf Robe Hunt (1905–77), a jeweler and member of Acoma Pueblo living in Tulsa, Oklahoma. He asked me to record certain Acoma sacred songs and prayers, because he believed he was the last tribal member to know them and he wanted them preserved. He feared they would be lost forever because Acoma youngsters no longer cared for traditional values and beliefs. I am pleased to say that after holding these recordings for more than twenty years in the Anthropological Archives they are now in the Acoma archives. Among the recordings I made for him was the Acoma scalp song. Upon hearing it, I expressed surprise because the Pueblo people are known for their pacifist ways. "True," Wolf Robe told me, "but we are a warrior people who have taken many scalps while protecting our homelands from invaders."

When did the Acoma take their last scalp? I asked. Wolf Robe thought a moment and then said, "For sure it was during the

Wolf Robe Hunt in his Acoma ceremonial clothing. Courtesy Herman J. Viola.

Second World War. I know my uncle took a German scalp. It was in the closing days of the war. He was a soldier in the US Army and he had been wounded during a fight to capture a city. He was lying semiconscious in a gutter along a street when two German soldiers walked past him. One of the soldiers gave him a kick to make sure he was dead. The kick jolted him to full consciousness. When he realized what had happened, he was so angry that he rolled over and tossed a hand grenade at the two soldiers, killing them both. Then he crawled over and scalped the one he thought had kicked him."

"Taking a scalp," Wolf Robe informed me, "carries responsibilities with it. The spirit of the person who has been scalped will always be hovering around, so my uncle had to take proper care of it. He had to feed it cornmeal and say the proper prayers so the spirit of the scalp owner did not harm him."

After hearing Wolf Robe Hunt's stories, I began asking other Native American friends about their military experiences, which they willingly shared with me. One of those friends, who later adopted me as his brother, was Joseph Medicine Crow, the Crow tribal historian at the time. Joseph, who died in 2016 at age 102, was descended from a long line of Crow war chiefs, including his grandfather Medicine Crow and his great uncle White Man Runs Him, who both aided the US Army during the Indian wars at the close of the nineteenth century. Joseph himself, as readers of *Warrior Spirit* have learned, served with distinction in World War II.

I first met Joe in the spring of 1973 when he visited the National Anthropological Archives. One morning my boss, Clifford Evans, chair of the Anthropology Department, called to ask a favor. "Herman," he said, "an old fraternity brother from my USC days has shown up unexpectedly and I am too busy to spend much time with him. He is a Crow Indian. I'll bet he would like to see some of the old Crow photographs in the Archives." A few minutes later Cliff showed up at my office with his fraternity brother in tow—a short, stocky, stern-faced, dark-skinned man in cowboy hat and cowboy boots.

After a few pleasantries, I asked Joe if he would like to see some Crow pictures. "I would like that," he replied. I left him in the research room with a stack of two hundred or so photographs and returned to my office. From time to time during the morning I observed him intently examining the photographs. As he neared the end of the pile, I asked him what he thought of the pictures. "I must say I am disappointed in them," he told me.

"Why?" I asked.

"Because you don't have a picture of my grandmother," he replied. As I started to tell him that we could not be expected to have a picture of every Indian who ever lived—it turned out his grandmother lived to be 105 and could speak five languages—he continued to examine the photographs and then stopped with a look of utter amazement on his face.

"What's the problem?" I asked.

"This picture cannot exist. I never saw it before."

The photograph of his family that Joseph Medicine Crow had never seen: his stepfather, John White Man Runs Him; John's wife, Amy Yellow Tail; and children Beauford and Arlis, 1923. National Anthropological Archives, Smithsonian Institution (BAE GN 06461a).

The photograph was of a handsome man and woman with two young boys. "That is my mother and father and my brothers," Joe explained. It turned out that the picture had been taken in the 1920s when a group of Crows came to Washington, DC, as part of a Shriner's rodeo. Joe recalled that he had stayed home to hunt and fish rather than make the trip with his family. One of the boys in the

Afterword

picture had since died, but his parents were still alive—in their seventies—and Joe asked if he could have a copy for his mother. Thus began my friendship with one of the most remarkable and unusual people I ever met. Eventually Joe and I did several books together, including *From the Heart of the Crow Country*, *Memoirs of a White Crow Indian*, and *Counting Coup*. The last-named book is the remarkable account of his World War II experiences.

Another Crow friend, Mardell Plain Feather, introduced me to Joe's nephew Carson Walks Over Ice, who had earned a Purple Heart, a Bronze Star, and a Silver Star for his heroics in Vietnam. When I mentioned to her my interest in meeting Native American veterans for a possible book about Indians in the military, she said, "Well, then, you will want to talk to my nephew Carson Walks Over Ice. He is a decorated veteran of the Vietnam War and his safe return was predicted in the Sun Dance. Everyone on the reservation knows that story."

Other Native veterans who shared their military experiences with me are Debra Kay Mooney, Chuck Boers, Ben Nighthorse Campbell, George Horse Capture, John Emhoolah, Vernon Tsoodle, Sam Stitt, Andrew Bird In Ground, and Henry Old Coyote. Their stories and others I heard and recorded over some thirty-five years working with American Indian veterans can be found in my book *Warriors in Uniform* (National Geographic Society, 2008).

The fitting capstone to this research came in 2015, when Kevin Gover, director of the National Museum of the American Indian, invited me to join his staff and assist in the creation of the National Native American Veterans Memorial. Although the US Congress had passed legislation authorizing its construction in 1994, final approval was not given until 2013. As the senior advisor to the project, my initial role was to assist in interviewing Native veterans and other members of the Indian community for their opinions, hopes, and possible concerns about the proposed memorial. At the conclusion of this two-year effort, I was then invited to serve on the eight-member committee that selected the winning design—by Harvey

Gina and Harvey Pratt with Herman and Susan Viola
at the annual Native American Veterans gathering at
Cantigny Park, Illinois, 2019. Courtesy Gina Pratt.

Pratt—from the 120 or so submissions received from across the
world. The dedication of the memorial, which is on the grounds of
the National Museum of the American Indian in Washington, DC,
was held November 11, 2020. Now, thanks to the memorial, the long-
overlooked patriotism, heroism, and contributions of American Indians to the armed forces of the United States will be commemorated
and honored into perpetuity.

In telling this story, I also wish to thank Barbara Brownell Gro-
gan and Kevin Mulroy for their invaluable assistance. I also thank
Stephanie Elaine Birdwell, VA Office of Tribal Government Rela-
tions; Joseph Craig, Association of the United States Army; Priscilla
Piestewa and Lorae (Homana) Pawiki; and my colleagues at the
National Museum of the American Indian, Kevin Gover, Elizabeth
Gordon, and Rebecca Trautmann, who invited me to help bring the
National Native American Veterans Memorial to reality.

Special thanks are due to Michelle Pearson and Cheryl Hughes, who created the Warrior Spirit Education Project and contributed essays to this book, and to Tim Steinouer, who has developed the project's classroom internet linkages.

Thanks are also due to the staff of the University of Oklahoma Press, especially Steven B. Baker and Alessandra Jacobi Tamulevich, and to indexer Chris Dodge.

My biggest debt of gratitude is to my wife, Susan, who welcomed the Indian interns into our home and who shared with me many and varied experiences during nearly four decades of travel across Indian Country.

Warrior Spirit: The Story of American Indian Heroism and Patriotism is a component of a K–12 education initiative inspired by the National Native American Veterans Memorial. Like the memorial itself, the goal of the Warrior Spirit education project is to provide students and teachers with information about the key roles Native American have played in our nation's military. The director of the project team is Dr. Herman Viola, curator emeritus of the Smithsonian Institution and senior advisor to the Veterans Memorial. His collaborators are Cheryl Hughes, an education consultant in Missoula, Montana, who is the project manager, and Michelle Pearson, a Colorado educator, who is the lead trainer and curriculum director.

The Warrior Spirit project presents the many ways Native people from hundreds of tribal nations have served in the US military and their reasons for doing so. The project has three themes. The first is to explore why American Indians have been in the forefront of our nation's military conflicts despite the fact that until World War II many tribal people were not fully enfranchised American citizens. The second is code talking, one of the most misunderstood topics related to American Indian military service. As readers of this book have learned, the fact that Navajos were Code Talkers during World War II is widely known. What is little known is that the use of tribal languages as a military code began in World War I and that soldiers from more than thirty tribes served in this capacity during these conflicts. The great irony, of course, is that our nation was forcing Native children to stop speaking their languages and learn English at the very time these languages were crucial to US military success. The third major theme is to introduce students and the public to Native heroes on and off the battlefield, such as those highlighted here in *Warrior Spirit*.

For more information, contact the Warrior Spirit Education Project at http://warriorsinuniform.com/Home.html.

Ellen Baumler earned her PhD from the University of Kansas and served a long career as interpretive historian at the Montana Historical Society in Helena until her retirement in 2018. She is a well-known storyteller and an award-winning author of many books and articles on a diverse array of Montana topics.

Cheryl Hughes has served as a 9–12 English teacher from Missoula, Montana, where she created a niche for her students in the world of place-based education. She also taught Native American literature and then joined an interdisciplinary freshman transition team that took students to the places and people whom the authors of their assigned literature wrote about throughout Montana. In 2016 she retired and began doing consulting work for educational programs of the National Museum of Forest Service History, the Montana Conservation Elders, and now the Warrior Spirit Project. Cheryl was as a Master Teacher for the NEH Landmarks "Richest Hills" workshops (2011, 2013, and 2014), cosponsored by the Montana Historical Society, and in 2015 was recognized by the Western Literature Association for her notable teaching in the Selway Bitterroot Wilderness.

Debra Kay Mooney is an Oklahoma native and a citizen of the Choctaw Nation of Oklahoma and of the Mississippi Band of Choctaw Indians. She has spent most of her time in church and involved with Native culture. In 1980 she was adopted, in the Indian way, into a Kiowa family, the Satepauhoodles. She has also been adopted into a Pawnee family, the Whites. Both families have given her permission to dance in their tribal clothes. During her college years she participated in Native American clubs and was a guest speaker in her classes when the subject was cultural diversity. She joined the Oklahoma National Guard in 1991 and was deployed overseas twice—in

2004 and 2008. During the 2004 deployment to Iraq, Sergeant Mooney and a few of her troops put together a powwow. Debra, who was invited to be an adviser for the National Native American Veterans Memorial, has spent her life in the pursuit of learning, teaching, and speaking about her culture.

Michelle Pearson is an educator and historic preservationist. She is half of the team Two Geeky Teachers and works in Adams 12 Five Star Schools in Thornton, Colorado. Pearson collaborates with local, state, and national partners to develop curriculum and resources for educators in history, historic preservation, Native American studies, and other content areas using primary sources and student-centered inquiry strategies. She has served as a volunteer for the Smithsonian Institution and the Department of the Interior, has served two terms as a White House Fellow in Education, and cofounded the Preserve America Youth Summit. She is the author of the books *Sacred Places of Denver* and *Historic Places of Denver for Children and Families* and was the 2008 Colorado Technology Teacher of the Year and the 2011 Colorado Teacher of the Year.